My Garden

Jacqueline van der Kloet

My Garden

A Year of Design and Experimentation

TIMBER PRESS
PORTLAND, OR

Timber Press
Workman Publishing
Hachette Book Group, Inc.
1290 Avenue of the Americas
New York, New York 10104
timberpress.com

Timber Press is an imprint of Workman Publishing, a division of Hachette Book Group, Inc.
The Timber Press name and logo are registered trademarks of Hachette Book Group, Inc.

Printed in China on responsibly sourced paper
Cover design by Sarah Crumb
Text design by Sarah Crumb, based on the original design by Volken Beck and Wouter Eertink

English translation: Kay Dixon, Expression Language Services
This edition based on a book originally published by HL Books, the Netherlands

The publisher is not responsible for websites (or their content) that are not owned by
the publisher.

ISBN 978-1-64326-456-1

A catalog record for this book is available from the Library of Congress.

CONTENTS

Jacqueline van der Kloet:
A Master Choreographer of Bulbs and Perennials

BY ROY DIBLIK

For most of my 70 years on this earth, 45 have been involved with perennial herbaceous plants as a propagator and grower. In the mid-1990s, I started designing native prairie gardens. Then, within a few years, I began designing all styles of perennial gardens using durable perennials and native plants. There is a certain gratification, continuing to be a *grower* of plants and at the same time placing them together socially through an articulated design. To understand the growing nature of plants and their collective ability to attract all forms of life, build soil and air, and live resourceful lives together is to be engaged in work that resonates on a vast scale, even when rooted in just one garden. Those of us involved in design practice and the evolution of planting processes continue to advance our inquiry on the inner workings of the world through the pursuit of knowledge around plants and plant relationships. This passion we share is driven by affection, curiosity, persistence, and continuous love from both the garden designer and the gardener.

With every gardening act there is a next moment. Designing with plants, like growing plants themselves, comes with similar qualities, one of which is making mistakes. And most of us understand that's how we learn; each mistake is two steps towards 'coming to know'.

Traditionally speaking, combining plants is often accomplished by mixing bloom dates, plant height, and flower colour along with cultural conditions. That typically satisfies what people want or expect to have as a garden—a place with plants that continue to bloom all year round. Unfortunately, plants don't care what people want. Simply having the awareness of plants but not knowledge of them limits the planting's purpose and longevity. It is not enough to *plant*, one needs to *understand* the processes behind the planting to achieve the deep, lasting effects of a beautiful, ecologically harmonious garden. The designer and gardener should know who the plants are, how they live, and how they can have dynamic and healthy lives in mixed-plant relationships. More traditional gardens fail to incorporate these interrelationships and therefore lose their integrity quickly, either getting replaced by new gardens or new building construction that gobbles up green space.

Change continually occurs in all ways of life and living. Naturalistic planting embraces this change and understands it as part of the garden's natural process. The availability and use of plants and evolving gardening practices are continuously moving forward. For me, and for many others I call collaborators and friends, gardens continue to be a visual art form combining the environment, ecology, food, and medicine and including all creatures, soil, and air in the process of creation.

More and more people from different fields of study are combining ecological and design practices, collaborating to create diverse plantings. We are coming to know plants as living, social beings that form intimate connections, as well as the deep importance of the connection between all living things. I have been fortunate to meet many people whose knowledge and actions are creating gardens that have transformed my way of understanding—people who question what and how we do something. It is the most forward-thinking visionaries who always seek to evolve their way of thinking and seeing. Jacqueline van der Kloet is one of these visionaries.

Twenty years ago, I had a planting experience that continues to resonate today. I met and worked with renowned naturalistic garden designer Piet Oudolf on the Lurie Garden in Chicago's Millennium Park. Piet created a wonderful change in my social thinking about plants. Because he let plants be themselves, the plant placement and community development in his designs were more fluid and truer to the plants' nature. I had seen this authentic expression in remnant prairies before, but never in gardening or landscape design. And along with the purposeful placement of plants that live well together, Piet Oudolf expressed the art of plant dynamics in relation to garden care, encouraging both health *and* beauty as essential to the garden's success. I knew what I learned that day was the beginning of a serious shift in my horticultural practice.

In 2005, the International Flower Bulb Centre donated about 30,000 bulbs to the gardens Piet Oudolf had designed in New York's Battery Park. Piet invited me out for the bulb planting. When I got to New York, he asked me to meet him for lunch at a restaurant just below the Brooklyn Bridge. When I got there two friends were with him: one was the director of the International Flower Bulb Centre, and the other was Jacqueline van der Kloet, whom Piet introduced as a bulb designing specialist from the Netherlands. I ate lunch wondering what that meant: 'a bulb designing specialist'. I will admit that I never used bulbs in my plantings at that time, and I had limited awareness of bulbs as anything other than masses of momentary entertainment, removed and replanted yearly in most gardens. In fact, I knew nothing of bulbs. In most gardens, there were always either too few bulbs scattered too far apart or so many I felt bombarded by a relentless tsunami of colour.

As I watched Jacqueline prepare herself to begin the bulb planting at Battery Park, I realized she was assessing the complexity of the plants already in the garden into which she was going to interplant the bulbs. This was a major feat: Jacqueline not only had to interpret Oudolf's diverse perennial pattens already in play—which meant both understanding sea-sonal growth rate and each plant's growth habits—she also had to work within the density of perennial plant development both seasonally and annually. I watched her work masterfully, placing groups of bulbs together within those already-complex patterns, and later witnessed them emerge and flower at different times, April through June, enhancing and never inhibiting the growth of the perennials around them.

Jacqueline took this complex process of interplanting bulbs with perennials and applied it in all the various patterns in Piet's design plan. It had become clear to me that I was witnessing an entirely new system emerging in horticulture. Jacqueline was using plants that I'd previously given little attention to; I had thought I was viewing bulbs in gardens at their best, but clearly this was far from the case. Witnessing Jacqueline's practice was a significant moment for me in my professional and personal development. I've always been influenced by the year-long seasonality of a plant, and suddenly bulbs had gotten my full attention.

In addition to a deep knowledge and understanding of plants, Jacqueline has a genuine way of working with people that makes the whole planting *fun*. At Battery Park, as she scattered handfuls of small bulbs placed casually within the plant groups, she would stop and start here and there, as if mimicking the way seeds drop in the wild, no handful the same—each bulb offering a layer of foliage and its own bloom time, flower size, and colour. Jacqueline tells stories with bulbs, each one a different language, engaging in a discussion with the diverse foliage of the perennials around which they emerge, whose textures, colours, and rate of growth echo the impressionistic bulb colours that pop up around them throughout the growing season. To see these two brilliant plantspeople interacting as if in a careful improvisation, speaking with plants, was mirrored in the expression of the plants themselves. First through Piet's and then Jacqueline's influence, I'm coming to know the full expression of a garden.

After this planting trip to New York those many years ago, I added bulbs to my list of 'come to know' plants. At that time, Jacqueline had a book out in the Netherlands presenting bulb combinations. When I received a copy of the U.K. edition, I began using her groupings within some of my perennial gardens. As I placed various bulb groupings using her technique, mixing varieties and types playfully, I realized it was hardly nonchalant. Jacqueline was emphasizing the importance of placing the bulb mixes with the perennial plants according to the proper rate of growth, as there is great nuance in their ability to complement each other. Jacqueline's knowledge of bulbs and bulb combinations also translates to her success designing perennial gardens. She's not just a bulbs designer, by any means.

The next year, the International Flower Bulb Centre donated about 60,000 bulbs to the Lurie Garden in Chicago. A Piet Oudolf planting, the Lurie Garden changed the possibilities of plants and the entire conversation around gardening in the United States at the time. After participating in New York's bulb planting the year before, I was excited to participate in whatever way I could. I knew something special was happening; Jacqueline van der Kloet was there to enhance and deepen a planting that was already loved and beautiful. Piet's Salvia River is the main feature of an everchanging garden that invites continuous emotional involvement, but Jacqueline's addition of the bulb layer provided an astounding deepening of texture and colour from mid-April to mid-June, adding yet another layer of beauty.

At the Lurie Garden, Jacqueline had an even more detailed plan than the one she had used in New York. This planting awakened the modern gardening eye to all the opportunities and possibilities of bulbs mingled with perennials. She highlighted the artful, dancing movement of bulbs as an opportunity to enhance the emerging colour and textures of the perennials. She had done it again: Lurie Garden is as pleasing as the wild beauty that occurs in the healthiest remnant landscapes in nature.

Jacqueline van der Kloet is a generous designer, a true collaborator, and a visionary. In these pages, she shares who she is as a plantsperson, designer, and gardener in relation to the plants she continues to come to know and love. Her deep knowledge of plants and how they interrelate is expressed in her designs of beautiful, diverse plant communities. For gardeners and designers working with plants, my hope is you'll experience Jacqueline's expert conceptual choreography, plant knowledge, and combinations of startling beauty, deepening your understanding of where and how you're asking plants to live. Jacqueline's planting practices will enable any gardener to celebrate a garden's health and beauty, bringing bulbs and perennials together in a dance of the four seasons.

INTRODUCTION

I am best known for my work with bulbs (and it's true, they *are* my favourite group of plants), but I grow many other plants in my own garden. I had been longing for years to make a book about what happens in a garden in 12 consecutive months. I wanted it to be a guide for readers to give them the feeling that they were being led by the hand to understand, step by step, the interaction between what you do in a garden and what the garden does to you. It is this synergy between practical details and instinctive experiences that I hope to share here—how one looks at the different seasons, for example, and how to learn to appreciate the beauty of each season.

Given that, apart from the work that I do as a garden and landscape designer and a plant specialist, I get huge enjoyment from my own garden into which I pour my heart and soul. And so it seemed obvious to write this book with my garden as the starting point. My garden is part of a historical area. When I came to live here in 1985, I started more or less from scratch, only integrating some existing trees, like the imposing line of black birch trees on the south side.

The wonderful thing about this garden is that it has a variety of biotopes: damp, fairly shady spots facing drier, very sunny places, and everything in between. That provides plenty of opportunities to experiment with combinations of plants that are adapted to varying conditions. In that sense, my garden is a breeding ground: I can try all sorts of things out here and monitor everything closely because I see all of it every day.

But this book covers more than just my own garden. There are also detours to other projects on which I worked, ranging from rather small private gardens in the Netherlands to large public parks, such as the Shinko Central Park in Yokohama, Japan, the Lurie Garden in Millennium Park, Chicago, Schloss Ippenburg in Germany, and, back in the Netherlands, the Keukenhof Gardens.

All in all, writing this book was great fun because, although it is not a diary, it does feel like gathering and arranging—in a pleasant way—all the experience and knowledge I have gained in this place throughout all these years. It has been an excellent means of looking at and experiencing my garden in a different way. Also, I had to take a lot of new pictures, and every time I looked through the camera I saw the garden in yet another, new way.

But, as always with living things, there were less-than-pleasant moments. Like when the black birch trees along the southern edge of the garden became diseased and died one by one. Or when the topiary box shrubs finally succumbed to a vicious moth in the late summer of 2018 and were stripped bare in no time. At such moments, my first reaction was panic, followed by acceptance, and then a kind of tension, because it means that the right choices have to be made to give the garden new balance in the future. It has been said countless times: A garden cannot be manufactured, and you can't force nature. It is the interplay of give and take and looking after each other that makes a garden so appealing to me.

This book is organised by month, beginning in September, and takes place over the course of one year. I have heard from many readers of the original Dutch edition that they started with the first chapter and read the whole book from there. Others started in the month in which they bought the book, and only started reading the next chapter when the corresponding month had arrived, because they wanted to know what was happening in the garden at that particular moment. Read it however you like. Or both ways!

I wrote these pages to share how I live with this garden and the inspiration it has provided me for projects all over the world. It is also a collection of technical gardening advice based on my own experience of more than 50 years of gardening—almost 40 of them in this specific garden. Those facts might be helpful for both the beginning and avid gardener, so everyone should take advantage of it in the way it suits you best.

For instance, you can pick a certain subject—like favourite plants—study all of those pages and, by submerging yourself in the various colours, structures, and foliage, develop your own favourite plant scheme. Or you could focus on spring-flowering bulbs as a starting point, only to discover a world of interesting facts that will be a great contribution to your general knowledge of bulbs, including the possibilities of using bulbs in containers and the best combinations. I also discuss trees for small gardens and seasonal borders with annual plants which instantly will make a good show in the same year in which they are planted. You'll find tips on watering, weeding, and cutting back at the right moment.

Photography plays a big role in this book. I'm particularly proud of the galleries featuring twelve fixed spots in the garden from month to month. I wanted to show how a garden develops and thrives throughout the year from the same vantage point. Gardeners are, quite often, incredibly visual thinkers!

My main goal is to celebrate my love of the garden with readers all over the world. I hope you enjoy it.

SEPTEMBER

In my mind, the most appropriate month to start with in a garden book is September. It's the month in which we start to take leave of summer, but at the same time preparations for spring can begin. I feel September is the month which makes it most obvious that 'the garden' is a continuous process, without a clear beginning or end. So if I have to choose where to start, then that would be September.

Goodbye, Summer

I used to suffer from September blues year after year: a feeling of despondency because the end of the garden season was looming and therefore work in the garden, and especially my enjoyment of it, would cease in the foreseeable future. But since I started writing this book and monitoring the changes in my garden much more intensively, that feeling has largely gone. Because September also brings hope: the first leaves of the grape hyacinths are already visible, and that lifts you over the dark winter months towards spring. This month makes it especially clear that you can't really talk about a garden season: it's a continuous cycle, and you can step into the garden at any moment and enjoy it because there is always a sign of new life somewhere. That's also why I certainly believe what

Blue grape hyacinths reveal their first leaves

an anonymous garden enthusiast once said, 'Garden people live longer because they are always looking ahead'.

September is also the month in which the first spiders' webs appear: sparkling works of art hanging on wispy threads in the most unlikely places. It is a month in which one and the same day can bring so many different forms of light. Soft morning light, which has a sense of mystery about it, is then wiped out fairly forcefully by the sun to make way for a much harsher midday light in which only bright colours hold their own: the warm yellow of *Coreopsis tripteris*, but also the magenta of *Geranium* 'Ann Folkard' and the shocking pink of *Erodium manescavii*. The *Gaura lindheimeri* tirelessly continues to flower and adds a graceful note to the garden in which more and more species are gradually going into their autumn phase: dried structures which, together with the box tree topiaries, will later be the distinguishing feature of winter.

A blue avenue for Martha Stewart

One of my first U.S. projects was linked to a famous name, Martha Stewart, the American entrepreneur, author, and television personality. It was the fall of 2010, and the idea was to create a blue avenue of spring-flowering bulbs beneath the established linden trees which line the entrance to her estate in New York's Westchester County. The project sprang from a television segment on blue bulbs that Martha did that October with the International Flower Bulb Centre—then the Dutch bulb growers and exporters' promotional organisation. They suggested Martha do a blue bulb planting in her linden allée and put me forward as the designer. I agreed, of course, and created an intricate mix of 122,000 bulbs with blue flowers, ranging from early-flowering to late-flowering varieties including *Crocus, Scilla, Chionodoxa, Anemone blanda, Muscari*, and *Hyacinthoides*.

That November I flew to New York together with International Flower Bulb Centre technical director, Frans Roozen. After an early wake-up call the next day, we set out to meet Martha. The early wake up was necessary

Shots from a television programme with Martha Stewart about planting bulbs

as Martha planned to film the planting for her television show and take photographs for a magazine article. It was quite an operation, with a large crew of filmmakers, writers, and photographers. Martha had a tight schedule that allowed only an hour for filming. There was a plane on standby to take her to her next appointment.

We had a very action-packed hour of making television. I showed Martha my 'scattering the bulbs' method, as Martha, Frans, and I were filmed and photographed. Martha was then rushed away to her plane, but she had arranged for an experienced crew to help with the heavy planting. Still we had our hands full for the rest of the day scattering and planting the bulbs, with more filming and photographing.

The result the following spring was even more stunning than we'd hoped: a sea of blue in a range of shades, flowering from the beginning of March to the end of April. Next came a very nice note from Martha and a fantastic article in her magazine, *Martha Stewart Living*, plus a television broadcast which was repeated several times.

The box tree moth

During the last year in which I was writing this book, the garden was attacked in September by an enemy I had feared for years: the box tree moth. I had seen the devastating damage this little moth can cause in all

The box tree moth larva, the great villain who devours all the leaves

kinds of other gardens throughout the country, but now it was our garden's turn.

The box tree moth is an invasive species which originates from East Asia and was first spotted in Europe in 2006. There's all sorts of well-meaning advice available to combat this moth with poison, organic or otherwise, but that always lands on other nearby plants too. And then other insects are killed unintentionally. So don't do it. The latest development is to use algae lime (high-quality lime from fossil sea algae) to combat it, but it is still too early to say anything useful about the results.

It was too late for our garden, in any case. The box trees were demolished in no time. There were scarcely 2 weeks between the moment I spotted the first moth to the end result (grey-brown, largely defoliated shrubs).

I felt complete panic at first, because some of the shaped box trees were over 40 years old. But because there was nothing to be done, we eventually resigned ourselves to it.

The fact that everything had to be replaced also presented a challenge. What now? The main thing was that it would have to be one or several species which would give the garden structure, especially in the winter, so preferably something evergreen. After having looked around at various nurseries, I finally made a decision I am very happy with. I have planted spherical *Osmanthus × burkwoodii* at a few crucial points; it is an evergreen holly-like shrub, which produces white flowers in spring. In the circular border where different sizes of box tree spheres used to be, I have now planted *Nandina domestica* 'Blush Pink', which is compact and rounded and turns a magnificent red in winter. Its common name is heavenly bamboo, but apart from that it bears no relation to bamboo. And the third species I have added is *Choisya × dewitteana* 'White Dazzler', an evergreen shrub which produces scented white flowers in April and May.

Before and after the unwelcome visit of the box tree moth

The loss of the box trees took a little getting used to, but the garden is certainly no less interesting as a result.

The hidden pond

The pond in our garden is invisible from the outside, but it is actually the centre of our garden. When the design for the garden was made in 1984, the idea was to create a walk around all the borders. The garden wouldn't be able to be seen completely at once, but you would keep discovering new parts of border. That was the reason for the decision to make an oval pond in the centre of the garden surrounded by a hedge. The hedge has created a hidden inner area which has a completely different atmosphere than the area outside the hedge.

The hidden inner space around the pond

Colchicum 'Waterlily'

We dug out the pond ourselves, to a depth of 1 m. Because of the heavy clay soil, it was an enormous task. Once the digging was done, we laid steel mesh to reinforce it, and finally the walls were coated in concrete. The finishing touch was an edge of old bricks which can also be sat on.

We have had plenty of problems with the pond over the years. The biggest problem was keeping the water clear. It fluctuated from crystal clear to green from algae, despite all the various water plants. After all sorts of experiments, we discovered that the imbalance was caused by a lack of oxygen. The solution, of course, was a pump, which we connected to a water feature we had been given by a good friend: a number of bronze butterbur leaves from which water bubbles. Since then, the pond has been crystal clear and therefore forms an attractive and surprising element in this central enclosed space. It is particularly special once the waterlilies and pickerel weed (*Pontederia*) flower, but even at other times of the year, the pond is a fine place to relax.

Autumn-flowering bulbous plants

It is always a surprise when the autumn-flowering bulbs appear. The first one to reveal itself in a few places which get lots of sun is always *Colchicum autumnale* 'Album'. But unfortunately, slugs love this species too. They nibble away at the emerging buds as soon as they can, and so the radiant white flowers—if they make it—end up with odd fringes.

A species which does develop well is *Colchicum* 'Giant' with its lilac flowers on 15-cm-tall stems. I explain to visitors to our garden every year what sort of bulbous plant it is and how you should treat it: plant *Colchicum* 'Giant' in August, and the flowers will appear immediately in September and October, followed by large, shiny leaves the following spring. It can then be left in the ground and will flower every year again, as long as it is in a damp enough spot which is not too dark.

Crocus speciosus 'Conqueror'

After this meadow saffron (the common name for *Colchicum*), the autumn crocuses follow at the end of September, beginning of October. We have one species, *Crocus speciosus* 'Conqueror', which is on the sunny side of a large beech tree in very dry soil. It's always wondrous to see the pointed buds popping up every year and watch them change into delicate little flowers in an improbable violet blue. If real autumn weather is forecast with wind and rain, your heart will be in your mouth, because they can't withstand that. Amazingly enough, the number of fine autumn days has been in the majority in the last few years, and under such circumstances these crocuses certainly flower for 2 to 3 weeks.

Planting snowdrops

Your head is still in the summer in September, but it's time to think far ahead again, because snowdrops have to be planted at the end of the month. That might seem early, but it is easy to explain. Snowdrops have a tendency to dry out after they are dug up. So it's a good idea to put them back in the ground as early as possible. That gives them the greatest chance of flowering in large quantities the following spring.

There are hundreds of different snowdrops, and some people do their best to collect as many different species and varieties as possible. We have three different species in our garden, and that's enough for me. When they flower en masse in spring they look enchanting—and you can create that look with 'ordinary' snowdrops just as well as with the more unusual species. So I stay loyal to *Galanthus nivalis* and its double snowdrop brother, *Galanthus nivalis* 'Flore Pleno', which both grow to a height of 10–15 cm, as well as the slightly taller (up to 20 cm) species *Galanthus elwesii*.

One of the more unusual snowdrop species, *Galanthus elwesii* var. *monostictus*

ORNAMENTAL GRASSES

I have experimented with a number of ornamental grasses in my own garden over the years. In the end, a few species remain which I am very satisfied with and which—by intervening once in a while—I can keep under control. The species which tend to seed profusely (*Milium effusum* 'Aureum', *Melica ciliata*, and *Nassella tenuissima* 'Pony Tails') are just as easy to remove again. The others require very little maintenance and do what they are supposed to do: add airiness to the border and attract attention at certain times due to their silhouette, the way in which they flower, or how their leaves change colour. And so, in this month in which most grasses are at their best, I have added an extra list below of favourite plants, devoted to ornamental grasses.

Acorus gramineus 'Ogon'
Anemanthele lessoniana
Calamagrostis × *acutiflora* 'Overdam'
Hakonechloa macra
Hakonechloa macra 'Albostriata'

Imperata cylindrica 'Red Baron'
Melica ciliata
Milium effusum 'Aureum'
Nassella tenuissima 'Pony Tails'
Pennisetum alopecuroides 'Hameln'

Hakonechloa macra

Milium effusum 'Aureum'

Nassella tenuissima 'Pony Tails'

Calamagrostis × acutiflora 'Overdam'

Imperata cylindrica 'Red Baron'

Golden rules

'Well begun is half done' goes the old saying, and that is absolutely true when it comes to planting bulbs and expecting them to perform at their best. My 30 years of experience in planting bulbs has resulted in a list of golden rules. These rules essentially are quite easy and will help you to make the best out of your bulb adventure.

RULE 1: ORDER ON TIME Once you have decided which bulbs are the most suitable ones in your situation, order them immediately to avoid the disappointment of certain species being sold out. Most gardeners wait too long and only start thinking about bulbs when it is almost time to start planting them, from September on. Too late! Make your bulb plan and bulb choices in spring and order after they have been harvested in June. At that point there still will be a wide choice and availability.

RULE 2: PROVIDE GOOD SOIL STRUCTURE Make sure that the soil in which the bulbs will be planted has good structure and is well drained. Most bulbs do not like getting their feet wet—but being too dry is not good either, because bulbs don't put down deep roots and so the soil needs to be able to retain sufficient moisture. The worst soil you can have is peaty soil because it normally is too wet all the time. In this kind of soil only moist-loving bulbs like *Fritillaria meleagris, Leucojum aestivum, Allium triquetrum, Allium ursinum*, and most daffodils will do rather well. Other soils like sandy soil and clay soil can be improved by adding compost (sandy soil) or compost and sand for extra drainage (clay soil).

RULE 3: STORE TEMPORARILY Once your bulbs have arrived, treat them with care. If you are not going to plant them right away, at least open the bags so that the bulbs can get enough air. Put them in a cool, dark, and dry place; 'cool' means in a place where the temperature does not exceed 12°C (54°F). If you have ordered bulbs that tend to dry out quickly, such as

Sorting the bulbs before planting

Allium ursinum, Eranthis, Erythronium, Fritillaria, Galanthus, Leucojum vernum, and *Lilium,* they need to be kept in a tray of sand or peat dust until they can be planted. Some other bulbs need soaking in water for a few hours, which helps them to get a good start: *Anemone blanda, Anemone coronaria, Eranthis,* and *Cyclamen.*

RULE 4: PLANT AT THE RIGHT TIME If you plant at the right time, it will help the bulbs to develop properly, they need to be able to form a good root system before the frost sets in. While the ground temperature is still between 5°C (41°F) and 10°C (50°F) that will happen quite quickly. An early night frost won't do too much damage if the topsoil thaws out during the day. Once the bulbs have rooted, they are frost-resistant, so no need to cover them. Early-flowering bulbs like snowdrops, star-hyacinth (*Scilla*), crocuses, winter aconites, *Erythronium* (dog-tooth violet), and anemones like to be planted early, ideally between late September and early October. From mid-October on you can plant daffodils and all remaining bulbs, with tulips, ornamental onions (*Allium*), and hyacinths being amongst the last ones to be planted. These require a colder soil, so plant them just before the frost sets in. After planting the bulbs you need to keep them watered well to stimulate root formation. So if there is no rain, water them yourself.

RULE 5: PLANT AT THE RIGHT DEPTH Plant the bulbs sufficiently deep: look at the height of the bulb and put twice as much soil on top of that: so a bulb with a height of 2.5 cm (1 inch) needs to be planted at a depth of 7.5 cm (3 inches), with 5 cm (2 inches) of soil on top of the bulb. If the bulbs are planted in sandy soil, they even need to be planted a little deeper to prevent them from drying out. Exceptions to this rule are *Lilium candidum* and *Cyclamen*; these species only need a very thin layer of soil on top.

RULE 6: DO NOT REMOVE THE FOLIAGE TOO EARLY All bulbs that are to be left in the ground to flower again the following year need to be given the opportunity to wither completely above ground in order to undergo their full growth cycle. That means that their leaves must not be cut off because those leaves provide the bulb with new nutrients. Time for a technical lesson: the leaves need to absorb light to convert the carbon dioxide in the leaves into carbohydrates, including glucose. This glucose is essential for the development of new buds in the following year. So do not cut (or mow, if the bulbs are in a lawn) the leaves before they have turned completely yellowish brown and dried out. The only exception here is the yellowing leaves of ornamental onions. They may be cut off straight away as this species of bulbous plant undergoes a totally different development.

RULE 7: APPLY SUFFICIENT FEED When you plant bulbs for the first time, there is no need to add compost because the bulbs contain enough nutrients to make it through the first season successfully. However, if you want your bulbs to naturalise or your tulips to perennialise, they need additional feeding from the second year on. In that case, use an organic ingredient, such as dried cow manure pellets. The best moment to apply this is in early spring, when the first green shoots appear above the ground.

RULE 8: DIVIDE BULB OFFSETS Bulbous plants that produce offsets (baby bulbs) need to have these baby bulbs removed from the parent bulb after a number of years and then be replanted. This will stimulate the growth of both the parent bulb and the baby bulb and give them all renewed energy for their next flowering season. This method is mainly the one to use for snowdrops, daffodils, crocuses, and *Camassia*. Snowdrops can also be divided immediately after flowering, while they are still 'in the green' (with green foliage), whereas June is the best time for all the other species.

12 Months in My Garden

JANUARY

FEBRUARY

MAY

JUNE

SEPTEMBER

OCTOBER

MARCH

APRIL

JULY

AUGUST

NOVEMBER

DECEMBER

Allium aflatunense

Favourite Plants: Lilac colour

Lilac is a colour that is torn between two others, sometimes tending towards violet and sometimes towards blue. It is a colour that does little on its own, needing the contrast and association with neighbouring plants. Next to deep purple and blue, lilac brings light and airiness. Next to scarlet, lilac serves to quench the fire a little. And there are no better combinations than that of lilac and deep terracotta, such as when *Aster × frikartii* 'Mönch' is partnered with *Cosmos atrosanguineus.*

Allium 'Gladiator'

Aster × *frikartii* 'Mönch'

Cleome 'Señorita Rosalita'

Colchicum 'Waterlily'

Geranium maculatum 'Elizabeth Ann'

Kalimeris incisa 'Blue Star'

Perovskia atriplicifolia

Thalictrum delavayi 'Splendide'

Vitex agnus-castus

OVAL BORDERS, ROTTERDAM

One of my projects involved creating a design for the redevelopment of a city square. The idea was to turn an unattractive paved area surrounding a church into an attractive place for visitors of the neighbouring cafés, restaurants, and shops. Because I had devised oval borders with raised beds, people would walk around, rather than through, the plants. I also wanted people to feel surrounded by greenery and to have a sheltered place to sit.

Designs for public spaces require low-maintenance plants. My plan involved interweaving recurring species of plants that would flower sequentially through the seasons and putting an emphasis on structures and plants that would look attractive in winter too. The final list of plants was limited to eighteen species of perennials (ten for the sunny borders and eight for the borders that get more shade), three species of shrubs, and a handful of spring-flowering bulbs.

The ovals are different sizes, varying from 10 m long and 4 m wide to 15 m long and 6 m wide.

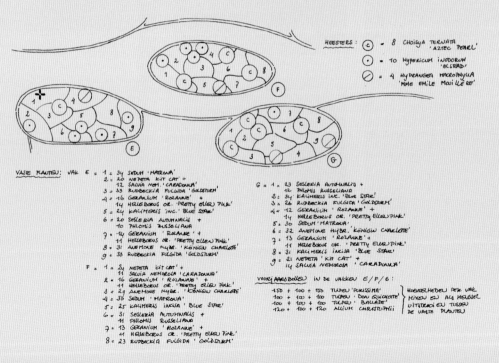

HEESTERS : (c) - 8 CHOISYA TERNATA 'AZTEC PEARL'
(·) - 10 HYPERICUM INODORUM 'ELSTEAD'
(⊘) - 4 HYDRANGEA MACROPHYLLA 'MME EMILE MOUILLÈRE'

VASTE PLANTEN: VAK E = 1 = 34 SEDUM 'MATRONA'
2 = 20 NEPETA KIT CAT +
   12 SALVIA NEM. 'CARADONNA'
3 = 33 RUDBECKIA FULGIDA 'GOLDSTURM'
4 = 16 GERANIUM 'ROZANNE' +
   14 HELLEBORUS OR. 'PRETTY ELLEN PINK'
5 = 24 KALIMERIS INC. 'BLUE STAR'
6 = 20 SESLERIA AUTUMNALIS +
   10 PHLOMIS RUSSELLIANA
7 = 14 GERANIUM 'ROZANNE' +
   11 HELLEBORUS OR. 'PRETTY ELLEN PINK'
8 = 31 ANEMONE HYBR. 'KÖNIGIN CHARLOTTE'
9 = 33 RUDBECKIA FULGIDA 'GOLDSTURM'

F = 1 = 24 NEPETA KIT CAT +
   11 SALVIA NEMOROSA 'CARADONNA'
2 = 16 GERANIUM 'ROZANNE' +
   11 HELLEBORUS OR. 'PRETTY ELLEN PINK'
3 = 29 ANEMONE HYBR. 'KÖNIGIN CHARLOTTE'
4 = 36 SEDUM 'MATRONA'
5 = 25 KALIMERIS INKISA 'BLUE STAR'
6 = 31 SESLERIA AUTUHNALIS +
   11 PHLOMIS RUSSELIANA
7 = 13 GERANIUM 'ROZANNE' +
   11 HELLEBORUS OR. 'PRETTY ELLEN PINK'
8 = 23 RUDBECKIA FULGIDA 'GOLDSTURM'

G = 1 = 23 SESLERIA AUTUHNALIS +
   12 PHLOMIS RUSSELIANA
2 = 34 KALIMERIS INC. 'BLUE STAR'
3 = 26 RUDBECKIA FULGIDA 'GOLDSTURM'
4 = 12 GERANIUM 'ROZANNE' +
   14 HELLEBORUS OR. 'PRETTY ELLEN PINK'
5 = 30 SEDUM 'MATRONA'
6 = 32 ANEMONE HYBR. 'KÖNIGIN CHARLOTTE'
7 = 13 GERANIUM 'ROZANNE' +
   11 HELLEBORUS OR. 'PRETTY ELLEN PINK'
8 = 31 KALIMERIS INKISA 'BLUE STAR'
9 = 21 NEPETA 'KIT CAT' +
   14 SALVIA NEMOROSA 'CARADONNA'

VOORJAARSBOLLEN IN DE VAKKEN E/F/6:
150 + 100 + 150 TULPEN 'PURISSIMA'
100 + 10 + 100 TULPEN 'DON QUICHOTTE'
100 + 100 + 100 TULPEN 'BALLADE'
120 + 100 + 120 ALLIUM CHRISTOPHII

} HOEVEELHEDEN PER VAK MIXEN EN AL MELDER UITTRECI EN TUSSEN DE VASTE PLANTEN

OCTOBER

More than 25 years ago, I was planting bulbs at the end of October when Karel, the little boy next door (who is now a very tall man in his 30s), came to ask me what I was doing. I had to switch to language he could understand and explained that I was putting little presents in the ground which would appear automatically in spring. And that all these funny-shaped, little balls which felt quite dry were called bulbs and that they would first go to sleep all winter long and would only wake up again when the sun started warming things up in the spring. He swallowed the story. After that, he regularly came to ask me how long it would be before the presents appeared above the ground. And that's how I feel every autumn: planting spring-flowering bulbs is like giving yourself a present you can have in a few months' time.

Foggy Days

Just as March can be full of surprises, the same applies to October. The first October in which I was writing this book was foggy, dull, wet, and chilly, although occasionally interspersed with one or two sunny days. Not exactly weather that invited me to go into the garden! But the next October, a year later, was a month with a lot of very nice days, relatively high temperatures, and only intermittent fog, which apparently is all part of its being October, but now with quite a different character. Where the last time the fog felt like an unpleasant damp blanket, it was now much more like a transparent veil that added a sense of mystery to the garden and dissolved as soon as the sun broke through.

Late flowers, autumn silhouettes, and autumn colours

The garden tries to make the best of it in October with late-flowering asters, autumn anemones, monkshood, wispy *Coreopsis tripteris*, and *Geranium* 'Ann Folkard', which never knows when to stop. I'm always surprised too by a plant which remains almost invisible all year but likes to show off its white flowers in October, brightening up the edge of the darkest border in our garden: *Saxifraga fortunei*. I can't understand how this seemingly so tender plant—which actually needs cool shade and a good damp soil with plenty of humus—can hold its own in our heavy, sticky clay and even survives being buried under an avalanche of wild garlic in the spring. A stayer I intend planting more of because, at this time of year, every bright spot is welcome. A second surprise in late autumn is *Crocus speciosus* 'Conqueror' which I mentioned last month, but I want to do so once again because its little ice-blue flowers are so touchingly sweet in amongst the now-bronze beech leaves.

Autumn silhouettes are something else which makes the garden interesting in October. When I make a planting plan, I always try to incorporate

Aconitum carmichaelii 'Arendsii'

Crocus speciosus 'Conqueror'

Imperata cylindrica 'Red Baron'

Geranium 'Ann Folkard'

Anemone tomentosa 'Robustissima'

Coreopsis tripteris

Saxifraga cortusifolia var. *fortunei*

Cladrastis lutea

Hypericum × inodorum 'Elstead'

Liriope muscari

Crataegus monogyna

Aster 'Treffpunkt'

Aconitum carmichaelii 'Arendsii'

as many plants as possible in it which are interesting even after they have flowered, due to their dried flowers, seeds, fruits, or distinct skeletons. There are all sorts of examples of this to be found in my own garden: the almost papery flowers of the hydrangeas; the fruits of *Hypericum, Kirengeshoma, Koelreuteria,* and *Aconitum*; and the play of lines of the taller ornamental grasses.

And the third aspect is the autumn colours which, although brief, are a commanding and distinctive feature. Especially on a clear day with a bright blue sky, the contrasting colours almost look artificial. Trees such as *Cladrastis lutea* (yellow-wood) and *Broussonetia papyrifera* (paper mulberry) radiate different shades of yellow, *Viburnum plicatum* var. *tomentosum* 'Nanum Semperflorens' swathes itself in rusty red, and the Juneberry tree (*Amelanchier*) almost looks on fire with its orange and scarlet leaves. One of the few ornamental grasses with a remarkable, ruby-red autumn colour is *Imperata cylindrica* 'Red Baron', Japanese blood grass. The greater the difference in temperature between that at night and the following day, the more intense the colours are.

My recipe for a natural effect is to mix bulbs and scatter them in the border.

Planting spring-flowering bulbs, part 1

But enough musing and philosophising. There is work to be done in October, for it's now the ideal month to plant spring-flowering bulbs. The best way of doing this is to stick to different planting times: the first half of October for crocuses and other bulbs that will naturalise, such as *Scilla* and glory of the snow (*Chionodoxa*), and the second half of October for daffodils. Plant tulips in November and *Allium* bulbs (ornamental onions) in December. If you want to plant mixtures of different species of bulbs, I recommend you choose a middle course and start at the end of October or beginning of November.

When we had just started laying out our garden in Weesp, tulips were the first bulbs to be planted in otherwise bare borders. Those tulips had been a gift: the remains of a large batch of tulips which had been used for an exhibition we had been involved in shortly before. With the image of that exhibition still in our minds, the tulips in our garden were planted in the same way: species by species, in roughly the same-sized strips. That produced a real spectacle of colour the following spring, and we were proud of it too. It's a good thing there aren't any photos of it, because my approach has changed radically over the years.

The current appearance of our spring garden, with alternating mixtures of varying sizes, emerged some 7 or 8 years after planting the garden—

actually by chance. At that time, in 1992 or thereabouts, I was writing
a monthly column for the Dutch magazine *vt wonen* about arrangements
of perennials in my garden. That column was also read by someone who
worked at the International Flower Bulb Centre, an organisation promot-
ing the Dutch bulb-growing industry at that time. This gentleman conse-
quently phoned me to ask if I would discuss the topic of spring-flowering
bulbs sometime. I answered completely truthfully that I had hardly any
experience with bulbs. He replied that something could be done about that.
I only needed to draw up a list of bulbs I would like to have, and then the
International Flower Bulb Centre would ensure that they would be delivered to me. He was true to his word, and the following year a large number
of crates of spring-flowering bulbs were delivered just as I had ordered.

In the meantime, I had been experimenting with perennials in various
combinations which always corresponded to the conditions of the spot they
were intended for and which were repeated here and there throughout the
garden to make it balanced. That worked well, and I decided to do the same
with the bulbs. And so I looked for bulbs that would suit each spot, made
a mixture of bulbs, and scattered them in amongst the perennials already
there. The result the following year exceeded all my expectations: never
before had I realised that you could recreate the same informal and natural
look of perennials with bulbs. Nor had I realised that bulbs and perennials
went together so well and even made each other look more attractive.

Crocus vernus
'Vanguard'

Ornithogalum
ponticum

Narcissus
'Elka'

Hyacinthus
multiflora
'Pink Festival'

Narcissus
'Thalia'

Allium
'His Excellency'

Leucojum
aestivum
'Gravetye Giant'

Part of this experiment was that I had decided to leave all the bulbs in the ground, even the tulips and some other bulbous plants which were reputed to be 'non-recurring'—time would tell what would happen. To my surprise, the majority of the planting reappeared the very next year. A few species did disappear after that, but they were then added to or replaced by newer ones. We are now 25 years on, and I still go through the garden every spring with a notebook, noting the places where more bulbs might be planted. And so every autumn, it's time to plant bulbs.

Winter protection

In the rare times that there is nothing more to be planted in the garden, I feel a sense of loss when I can't plant bulbs. That is why I regularly plant spring-flowering bulbs in pots too. What you need to think about then is protecting them in winter: if it turns really cold, bulbs in pots are more vulnerable than those in the ground; the cold gets in through the sides of the pot and then there is a great risk of freezing. So don't place the bulbs too close to the edge of the pot and, just in case, wrap the pot up too. I often wrap blister padding around the pot, but I have also experimented with placing the pot of bulbs in a large steel-mesh basket and then filling up the space around it with fallen leaves. I do that every year with a pot of *Agapanthus*, and that's been successful up to now.

A blanket of leaves as protection against the impending chill of winter

Plants I regret planting

One of my fundamental principles when making a planting plan is only to use plants I know well: I know how they will behave and what they will look like in the growing season. But many years ago, at the time when the

Some species are suitable for filling a large area, but once you've got them, they're difficult to get rid of. From left to right: Bluebells, wild garlic, and *Ranunculus psilostachys* which looks a bit like buttercups.

borders in our garden had to be filled one by one, I allowed myself to occasionally be tempted by a pretty picture in a catalogue or by recommendations from a garden centre. And so some plants entered our garden in the early years which, with hindsight, I now bitterly regret.

Some of these plants turned out to be very stubborn and hard to get rid of. One of them, which I mention elsewhere in this book, is *Allium ursinum*, wild garlic. It is magnificent when in flower, but impossible to keep in check. The fleshy bulbs are difficult to remove from greasy clay soil, exacerbating the problem. Other species that weave their way in between other plants in no time and are almost impossible to get rid of are *Allium triquetrum* (three-cornered garlic), *Anemone canadensis* (a sweet little flower but it spreads aggressively), and *Houttuynia cordata* 'Chameleon'. I had planted the last of these in the smallest border, surrounded by gravel, assuming that it couldn't do too much damage there. But after years of irritation, I finally dug up the whole border and sieved the soil as best I could to get rid of any last bits of rootstock. Even now I still find little shoots here and there.

Less aggressive and slightly easier to get rid of are *Lysimachia punctata*, *Ranunculus psilostachys*, and *Anemone tomentosa* 'Robustissima'. The first two have now pretty well disappeared from my garden, but I still keep a close eye on the places they used to grow. I am still battling with the last one. Regardless of how pretty this plant is when it flowers, it pushes out all the other plants after a while. And that detracts from the balance, so it has to go.

12 Months in My Garden

JANUARY

FEBRUARY

MAY

JUNE

SEPTEMBER

OCTOBER

MARCH

APRIL

JULY

AUGUST

NOVEMBER

DECEMBER

BULBS IN POTS, TUBS, AND BASKETS

Even when you do not have an actual garden, but only a roof terrace, a balcony, or a tiny courtyard, you still can look forward to the arrival of spring by planting spring-flowering bulbs in all kinds of containers. Almost anything can be filled with bulbs, and if you do this right they will give you a lot of pleasure in the following season.

And it is all very easy, though bulbs in containers do require some care. You can't just put a few bulbs in a pot, set it aside until spring, and then expect a wonderful result. Just take one step at a time and simply start by choosing the right container. That means it has to be big enough so there is no risk of the bulbs drying out in too little soil. A good size to start with is a container of at least 25 cm (10 inches) both in height and diameter. The sides of the pot should not be too slanting because if they are, the outer bulbs will hardly be in any depth of soil. And an absolute necessity is to have a hole in the bottom of the pot to allow excess water to drain away.

The pot should not freeze in the meantime, either. In that case there is the choice of plastic pots, cement ones, wooden planters, or earthenware pots that are lined on the inside with insulating blister padding. That insulation prevents the pot from absorbing liquid from the soil, so the pot stays drier and there is less risk of cracking when the pot freezes. What I do regularly is fill plastic containers with bulbs and then place them in a slightly larger, nice-looking stone container. That looks attractive and there is virtually no chance of the stone pot cracking when it freezes.

Step two is thoroughly cleaning the container and putting a layer of clay granules or shards of broken pots on the bottom. That layer ensures that surplus rainwater or water from the watering can easily drain away. Bulbs hate sitting in wet soil! Then put a layer of potting compost on top; the layer should be at least 10 cm (4 inches) high. Then add the bulbs—not too close to one another and not too close to the edge of the container because frost can penetrate the sides of the pot. Finish it off by putting potting compost on top of the bulbs, until the container is full. Water the container regularly in the first 2 weeks after planting the bulbs to make sure that they make roots as soon as possible.

Bulbs in pots at ground level sometimes can be damaged by mice. To prevent that, stretch some fine-mesh gauze over the pot. Then find a good spot to help the potted bulbs survive the winter. Ideally, you want them to experience the most natural winter conditions. So don't put them in the garage or in a shed because it will be too dry there and, as spring arrives, too dark. The best place is a sheltered

spot outside: against a wall or a fence. Put all the pots together after having wrapped each pot in insulating blister padding and then put an old plastic tablecloth around all of them. I have tried it this way, and it worked pretty well!

If you are putting bulbs in pots for the first time, it's sensible to start with one species that never fails. So, for the beginners: you can't go wrong with crocuses. They are amongst the first ones to flower, and they come in all kinds of colours. Although crocuses are very easy bulbs for containers, they absolutely need a place in the sun and, unfortunately, they will not flower very long—no longer than 10 days. Dwarf daffodils might be a better choice, though they flower a little later but definitely longer: *Narcissus* 'Jack Snipe' (white and yellow) and *Narcissus* 'Jetfire' (yellow and orange) are strong varieties that do very well in pots. A little later in spring there is a wide choice of grape hyacinths; they always perform well in containers. All of these species and varieties need little care. Just make sure that they get some water from time to time.

If your first trials with bulbs in pots have been successful, the next year you might be motivated enough to take step two and plant bulbs in pots in more than one layer. We call that the sandwich or lasagna system, in which various species of bulbs are planted in layers one on top of the other. You will achieve the nicest result if you choose species that bloom in a sequence of flowering periods, so for instance crocuses for early season, grape hyacinths for mid-season, and wild tulips for late season or glory of the snow (*Chionodoxa forbesii* 'Blue Giant') for the early period, miniature-daffodils like *Narcissus* 'Elka' or 'Tête-à-Tête' for mid-season, and lily-flowered *Tulipa* 'Ballade' for the latest part of spring. A constant succession of flowers for at least 4 or 5 weeks!

Basically, the sandwich system works the same. You'll need a container that is large (and high!) enough to host three layers of bulbs, a hole in the bottom with shards on top, and a first layer of at least 10 cm (4 inches) of potting compost. And from here you have to pay attention because the *first* layer of bulbs should be the ones that flower as the *last* ones in the season. Make a nice layer of them, not putting them too close to one another (the bulbs should not touch each other) and cover them with potting compost until you can't see the top of the bulbs anymore. Then put in the second layer of bulbs: the ones that flower in mid-season. Again, cover them with potting compost until the top of the bulbs is totally covered. Then comes the *last* layer, the bulbs that will flower as the *earliest* ones. They probably will be small bulbs like crocuses, blue or white squill, or anemones, so they only need a cover of 5–7 cm (2–2.5 inches). The possibilities of combining various species in a container are endless and the results are always surprising. Make yourself a bouquet of spring-flowering bulbs that will last for weeks!

Camassia quamash

Favourite Plants: Purple

If you take a broad view of the various colours of flowers throughout the year, it is striking how much white and yellow there is in spring, whereas autumn depends more on the deeper shades such as strawberry pink and purple. These are colours which reflect the warmth of the sun. Therefore, late-flowering plants or those which flower for a long time are in the majority in my list of favourite purple-flowered plants:

Ageratum houstonianum 'Red Sea'

Geranium × *magnificum*

Liriope muscari

Lobelia speciosa 'Tania'

Phlox paniculata 'Düsterlohe'

Salvia nemorosa 'Caradonna'

Salvia viridis

Verbena bonariensis 'Lollipop'

Veronica longifolia 'Marietta'

NOVEMBER

I regularly work on projects abroad. It's always interesting to see how people work in other countries, certainly when their way of working is very different than ours. For example, once I was in Yokohama, Japan, where I had been asked to help with the redevelopment of a city park. I had made suggestions before I got there, and work on them had already started. I arrived to check on things but also to plant bulbs. When everyone was ready at eight o'clock in the morning, all the people involved formed a circle. The purpose of that was to listen to a pep talk about the programme for the day from a representative of the municipal parks department; the attendant firm of landscape architects; the contractor; a technical lady who would be available to answer any questions about coffee, lunch, and toilet breaks and the wearing of protective clothing; and—to my surprise—me. The same happened at the end of the day, but then as a review. Quite extraordinary to experience!

Structures and Silhouettes

Every year, between September and the end of November, I give a few lectures on combining flower bulbs and perennials, but also on the technical aspects of planting bulbs. There are invariably all sorts of questions at the end of the lecture, mainly about tulips: why they don't come up, why they don't return every year, and—periodically—why it is that they produce red flowers in their first year and yellow the second year. That last one is wondrous to me, too, but to reply that the questioner is probably mistaken is of course not an option. What many garden enthusiasts, even the very experienced ones, don't realise is that tulips are not the easiest of bulbs. But if you take the right measures, you will still have a good chance of success.

Tulips originate from the bare high mountains of Central Asia. They definitely need a sunny position in a well-drained spot that remains sufficiently warm and dry in the summer so that the flower-producing bulb can develop as well as possible in time for the next spring. Tulips' greatest enemy is automatic irrigation systems which make the soil damp and cool

in summer. Furthermore, tulips need to be planted deeply enough, at least 15 cm (6 inches) deep. At the end of their flowering period, they must be given the chance to collect sufficient nourishment for next year's young bulb to enable it to develop a flower independently. That nourishment partly comes from the plant itself, where carbohydrates in the leaves and stem are converted into sugars, and partly from additional, preferably organic, compost.

Apart from all this, the time when tulips are planted is also important: tulips planted too early in the season in soil which is too warm are more susceptible to diseases than tulips planted later in cooler soil. The ideal soil temperature is between 5 and 10°C (41 to 50°F), that is, in November!

Tulipa
'Ballerina'

Tulipa
saxatilis

Tulipa
'Flashback'

Tulipa
'Peppermint Stick'

Tulipa
tarda

A large project needs hundreds of bulbs   Grasses tied together to make room for scattering bulbs

This is the most important reason why I prefer to plant in November: it helps to exclude a risk. The other reason to plant bulbs in November is that in October, the garden is often still looking wonderful and it would be a shame to start cutting plants back at that time. And that is something you really have to do, because while it might sound easy to scatter bulbs in amongst perennials, in practice, you'll never find them all again if you don't cut the surrounding perennials back first.

In one of the projects I worked on abroad, large numbers of bulbs had to be planted in October because winter comes early in the region. It was in the Lurie Garden in Millennium Park in Chicago to supplement the planting plan of perennials and ornamental grasses that Piet Oudolf had made for the garden. That posed a dilemma for us because autumn was exactly the time the garden looked magnificent with its large quantities of ornamental grasses. Cutting them all back was obviously out of the question, but randomly scattering the 60,000 bulbs that were needed amongst the luxuriant perennials and ornamental grasses wasn't an option either. Thanks to a group of fifty volunteers, Friends of the Lurie Garden, it all worked out well in the end. They tied vast quantities of grasses together and cut some perennials back here and there which were not so essential for the winter look. That enabled us to put in the bulbs fairly easily, in a way that left them visible for the people who were actually going to plant them.

Lurie Garden in Millennium
Park, Chicago

Cosmetic maintenance

Once the bulbs are in the ground, I always do a round of cosmetic mainte-nance. That means that I get the garden looking as good as possible before the winter. I cut off broken or snapped-off stems, and I usually remove the trailing leaves of the *Hosta* too, since it doesn't provide much protection anymore. Tidying up like this makes a big difference: the distinct silhou-ettes and structures that emerge seem to bring the garden back to life. It is pleasant to look at, and when frost or a light covering of snow adds an edging of silver, you'll be glad you put in that effort.

After that, it's time to rake over the gravel paths. The reason that is so important is something I only understood when I made a garden plan for a friend who had gone to live on a farm with lots of gravel around the house. That gravel was raked every Saturday, not just to make it look tidy for the following day, but to rake up any seedlings which have lodged in the gravel.

And there are plenty of seedlings around in November: the forget-me-not is proudly showing me that I can expect lots of flowers next year, but I prefer not to have these seedlings in the gravel. Sometimes I move a few to the adjoining borders or even into the pots filled with bulbs, but the rest go on the compost heap. The golden wood millet (*Milium*) has also left a trail of seedlings all over the gravel. I take them all out, because this little

Hydrangea macrophylla 'Madame Emile Mouillère'

No need to get rid of the autumn leaves

The trunk of *Prunus serrula*

Dried flower heads of *Allium nigrum*

Aconitum carmichaelii 'Arendsii'

Lunaria rediviva

The plumes of
*Pennisetum seta-
ceum* 'Rubrum'

plant has already seeded itself profusely in the borders. That concludes the work outside for this month, allowing me to concentrate on different garden things.

Spring-flowering bulbs in other countries

At the beginning of this chapter, I wrote about the projects in other countries that have occasionally crossed my path. I tend to visit them in autumn when the spring-flowering bulbs need to be planted. I spent 2 weeks in Japan in November 2016 for a project in Yokohama and another in Nagasaki. I was invited to Yokohama because a Japanese landscape architect, who had worked on the Japanese pavilion at Floriade 2012, had noticed my spring plantings at that Floriade. She was so impressed that she arranged an assignment for me in Yokohama. That assignment was to renovate an existing small park close to the harbour and to plant spring-flowering bulbs followed by annuals in connection with a green event, the National Urban Greenery Fair, in spring 2017. After my first visit in May 2016, when I took notes and photos, I had to make a proposal for replanting the park and for the additional planting.

The original planting was hopelessly old-fashioned, with far too many species, different species of plant in every spot, and no interconnection at all. I had to put a lot of thought into it but when I arrived the second time, in November, the whole thing looked reasonably good. After a few final adjustments, it was time to plant mixtures of bulbs. That was a very special moment for all concerned because up until then bulbs had been planted here in clusters of the same species, randomly spread over the borders. There was a large group of enthusiastic volunteers ready to help with scattering and planting the bulbs. After I had explained briefly what I wanted and demonstrated what I meant, they all dived into the crates of bulbs.

Spring and early summer in
Shinko Central Square

I had to step in then, because when the bulbs were being scattered they were flying about all over the place. But after working hard for 4 days, the job was done and I flew on to Nagasaki for the second project.

A theme park has been built there covering an area of 2 km² and given the Dutch name Huis ten Bosch. The park contains replicas of famous Dutch buildings and locations, such as the town hall in Gouda, Amsterdam Central Station, the Dom cathedral tower in Utrecht, and the Passage in The Hague, all meticulously copied on a scale of 1:1. Add to that the Kinderdijk windmills and Hotel de L'Europe where I was staying and you have a collection of atmospheres that is rather alienating but which also has a certain charm. The Japanese and inhabitants of surrounding countries love it, and hundreds of thousands of visitors arrive each year. The park celebrated its twenty-fifth anniversary in 2017, and, in honour of that, I was asked to design a plan for bulbs in the front garden of Huis ten Bosch Palace, which had also been given a place there. My design was fairly simple: tulips in different mixtures of colours, laid in strips, alternated with strips of mixtures of biennial spring flowers such as forget-me-nots, wallflowers, and *Bellis*. For an area of over 300 m², that meant that tens of thousands of bulbs had to be put in the ground. Helped by a garden team of fifteen men and women, the job was done in 3 days.

The results of both projects were very satisfying. The project in Nagasaki was the easiest because they wanted a once-only sea of colour. After an initial cold start, all the tulip bulbs and biennials did tremendously well, resulting in a succession of different colour combinations lasting 3 weeks. The visitors—who were used to seeing small areas mainly containing previous years' yellow and red tulips—were very appreciative. The bar was set a bit higher in Yokohama: here the spring flowers produced by the various bulbous plants had to be succeeded by just as lavishly flowering perennials and annuals and after that, following the usual rainy season in June and July, by a combination of autumn-flowering perennials and ornamental grasses. Luckily the weather gods were on our side, everything went according to plan, and the park became more and more beautiful as

It took a team of fifteen gardeners and 3 days to plant 60,000 tulip bulbs in the front garden of Huis ten Bosch Palace in Nagasaki.

time went on. Everyone was so pleased with it that the organisers decided to continue the project—which had been intended as a one-off—the following year. And so that is how Shinko Central Park has now become a little green gem on the edge of the centre of Yokohama.

In Europe, Germany is a constant factor for me because I am very frequently asked to do assignments there. I started back in 2003 with plans for Schloss Ippenburg in Bad Essen, near Osnabrück. Different bulbs were planted every year, and the high point came in 2010 when one of the national garden festivals (*Landesgartenschau*) was held in the town. My last project there was in 2016, because after that the castle was handed over to the son of the house, who unfortunately wanted to chart a completely different course.

Spring at Schloss Ippenburg

Gräflicher Park in Bad Driburg

I was asked to plant bulbs in Bad Driburg in Germany—where Piet Oudolf had made gigantic borders for the Gräflicher Park—as a forerunner for the exuberant perennials in the summer. One of my plans was also implemented in the Botanic Gardens in Gütersloh: a mixed planting of spring-flowering bulbs and biennials in the parterres of its English Garden. I am mostly present when these projects are planted, and the experience is always different and special. This type of work mainly keeps me busy in October and November. That means that my own garden has to take a back seat for a little while, but I don't worry about it because there isn't so much to do in the garden at this time of year. These foreign assignments are very inspiring, but when I return home at the end of November and see the first flowers appearing in my *Viburnum* × *bodnantense* 'Dawn' in my own garden, I'm always pleased to be home.

12 Months in My Garden

JANUARY

FEBRUARY

MAY

JUNE

SEPTEMBER

OCTOBER

MARCH

APRIL

JULY

AUGUST

NOVEMBER

DECEMBER

Senecio cineraria 'Cirrus'

Favourite Plants: Grey and Brown

November symbolises a range of shades of grey: it is a largely colourless month. The plant world has many shades of grey, which are mainly found in leaves. This grey is everything but colourless and dull because it comes in various subtle distinctions: silvery green, silvery white, or tending more towards blue. Grey-leaved plants are indispensable in leafy borders where a lighter accent is needed or alternatively in very colourful borders to give the border some breathing space. But grey can also marry well with a neutral colour such as white: just think of the white garden at Sissinghurst, where grey-leaved plants play a prominent part and do so with verve! The colour brown is also a late-fall colour and a good companion to grey, though most of the brown species are at their peak earlier than November:

Amaranthus cruentus 'Hot Biscuits'

Eryngium yuccifolium

Eucomis comosa 'Sparkling Rosy'

Euphorbia myrsinites

Pennisetum macrourum

Pennisetum 'Vertigo'

Ratibida columnifera

Salvia farinacea 'Cirrus'

Salvia officinalis 'Purpurascens'

DECEMBER

The winters when I was young were definitely colder than they are now: biting winds in November and long walks in deep snow on Christmas Day. This year, a stray yellow *Verbascum* was still flowering in the gravel in mid-December, while around the corner, at the café along the River Vecht, customers were enjoying their coffees outside. That's the surprising thing about nature: no year is the same, but this time the climate really looks as though it is changing.

Hibernation ... or Not?

The effects of climate change can also be clearly seen in one of the few species of perennial that flowers in our garden in the winter, *Helleborus* or Christmas rose. It certainly lives up to its name because from the end of October, fat buds start appearing on *Helleborus foetidus* (stinking helle-bore) which usually change to apple-green flowers before Christmas. That has indeed happened now, but in addition fat buds were appearing on *Helleborus orientalis* too—quite unusual—because this species doesn't usu-ally flower until February in a normal winter.

As soon as flowers appear, that is the right moment to cut away the evergreen leaves so that you can see the flowers better. But at the same time it is an effective means of combating leaf spot which occasionally afflicts hellebores. And now I found myself going around with the shears on a pleasant, spring-like day in December. It's very easy to cut away these leaves because, although they stand upright almost all year, keeping the heart of the plant in shadow, they fall sideways at the time the buds are forming. It's as though the leaves of the plant are trying to say: 'We're mak-ing room for the buds to grow and we're ready to be cut off.' And then they form a wreath of leaves on the ground and you can see exactly where you need to cut.

All hellebores do well in the rich humid clay soil in our garden. It takes a while before the young plants get real volume, but once they are settled,

Speckled *Helleborus orientalis*

New buds appearing on *Helleborus orientalis*

Frost makes the plants collapse . . .

But not for long.

Crushed eggshells provide extra lime.

Helleborus × *hybridus* 'Pretty Ellen White' in full flower

Forget-me-not seedlings in the gravel path

they sometimes even produce twenty flower stalks per plant. What certainly helps are the crushed eggshells I scatter around them, because hellebores really like lime. They are very resilient too, because they survive fairly cold periods without any problem even though it sometimes doesn't appear so. When they start bending over with floppy stems, you fear the worst. But when the temperature rises once more, they proudly stand up again in no time! Hellebores' long flowering season of at least 8 weeks is very appealing too; and they even look attractive when forming seeds. An ideal winter plant!

Hellebores come in all sorts of colours and shapes, but my favourites are the simple white or greenish pink ones because these colours stand out against the mostly dark winter background. The many cultivars in my garden have now produced all sorts of seedlings. If I had to choose a pretty hellebore for one of my client's gardens, my choice would be *Helleborus* × *hybridus* 'Pretty Ellen White'; and there are also variants in pink and claret with—of course—corresponding names such as 'Pretty Ellen Pink' and 'Pretty Ellen Red'.

Winter annuals

Another sign of life in our winter garden emerges in the form of winter annuals: little plants that bear this name because they are active in winter. They follow a cycle of flowering in spring or early summer, forming and disseminating seeds immediately after they have flowered, after which the seeds germinate in autumn and immediately form evergreen basal rosettes. Because of the chemicals in their leaves, such as raffinose, these basal rosettes can withstand frost and they survive the winter unscathed. The rosettes stand out straight away in the bare winter garden which makes it easy to see where they have spread. Forget-me-nots, in particular, tend to give themselves away by nestling in the dozens in the edges of the gravel along the borders. It is then simple to remove them from places where you don't want them to grow.

As soon as the temperature starts to rise in March, winter annuals develop rapidly and grow into familiar spring- and early-summer-flowering plants such as *Bellis* (daisy), *Alcea* (hollyhocks), *Myosotis* (forget-me-not), which I mentioned before, and *Digitalis* (foxglove). The term *winter annuals* is therefore nothing more than another word for biennials. But apart from that, they are unmistakable heralds of a new garden season and therefore points of light in the dark winter months. These months don't have to be spent indoors all the time, incidentally, because now that the climate is becoming milder, there are always jobs to be found that can be done outdoors.

Planting spring-flowering bulbs, part 2

December, for instance, is an excellent month for planting certain bulbous plants. Some species actually prefer to be planted later in the season, including tulips, *Camassia* (camas or Indian hyacinth), *Anemone coronaria* (garden anemone), *Allium*, and *Nectaroscordum* (honey garlic). The choice is of course limited at that time, but there are enough companies selling off their last remaining bulbs at the end of the season. And then you can sometimes seize your chance. It's best to choose a company that has kept its bulbs in good conditions after they have been dug up, that is, cooled correctly. That's because the quality of bulbs will have deteriorated rapidly if they have lain in too-warm and dry conditions since the end of August, as happens in several large garden centres.

I always plant most of the larger bulbs (tulips, *Camassia*, *Nectaroscordum*, and daffodils) using a special bulb planter: a tube with a long handle that you screw into the ground. After that, you pull the handle out again so that the soil stays in the tube, leaving a decent hole for the plant at just the right depth. Admittedly, this only works on clay soil and loamy sandy soil. If the soil is too loose, you won't be able to make such a nice deep hole and you'll still have to go in there with a trowel.

Tulipa 'Flaming Parrot'

Using a bulb planter for larger bulbs

I have always tried to work as sustainably as possible when planting bulbs. I don't plant them every year and then dig them up again after they have flowered, try to store them, and then eventually buy new bulbs again. Instead, I plant them, leave them in the ground after they have flowered, and then hope that they will flower again for many years. That method works well for several species, but tulips are always a risk. That is because they are very particular, needing the right habitat, not too wet and not too dry, the right amount of light, and various other requirements. Experience has taught me that the strongest tulips—which are likely to flower for several years—come from the groups of Darwin hybrids, lily-flowering tulips, a few late tulips, and double-late tulips. But there are a number of parrot tulips, including *Tulipa* 'Black Parrot', 'Flaming Parrot', and 'Professor Röntgen' which will return several years in succession too.

A surprisingly high percentage of ornamental onions last for many years as well. Groups of *Allium nigrum* (a misleading name, because the flowers are white with a green heart) have flowered profusely for more

Allium aflatunense
'Purple Sensation'

than 20 years in a border in my garden that isn't even in full sun. They open just at the time the white lily-flowering tulips 'White Triumphator' in the same border are dying back and so one perfectly replaces the other. Other *Allium* species that last for many years and sometimes even spread annoyingly can be found in the following list:

Allium aflatunense 'Purple Sensation' (purple)

Allium cowanii (Neapolitan garlic, white)

Allium 'Firmament' (amethyst)

Allium moly (yellow)

Allium oreophilum (rose-pink)

Allium roseum (pink)

Allium sphaerocephalon (drumstick, claret)

Allium triquetrum (three-cornered garlic, white)

Allium ursinum (wild garlic, white)

Nectaroscordum siculum (honey garlic, creamy green)

Nectaroscordum siculum

Camassia leichtlinii 'Caerulea'

Tulipa 'Ballerina'

Tulipa 'Daydream'

Mixture of tulips and *Anemone coronaria*

Tulipa 'Marilyn'

Allium triquetrum

Allium ursinum

The camas or Indian hyacinth (*Camassia*) is a species unfamiliar to most people. When they are in flower, though, they are very striking and then everyone wants this bulb in their garden. I saw them first in Christopher Lloyd's flower meadows at Great Dixter and was immediately captivated by them: stately pale blue, bright blue, and now also creamy white flowers growing to a height of about 80 cm. They are in my garden in both full sun and partial shade, and they do equally well in either. That is partly because of the rich and somewhat damp soil they are in. The most well-known are *Camassia cusickii* (ice-blue), *Camassia leichtlinii* 'Caerulea' (bright blue) and *Camassia leichtlinii* 'Sacajawea' which has creamy white flowers and leaves edged in white. Apart from these tall species, there is also *Camassia quamash* (bright blue) which grows no taller than 40 cm.

And then you have the poppy anemones or windflowers, a product that is becoming increasingly interesting because of the changing climate. When I started planting bulbs over 30 years ago, anemones were designated as 'not winter hardy', but nowadays I'm quite prepared to plant them out. *Anemone coronaria* 'Sylphide' (violet) and 'Mr Fokker' (dark blue) grow at the edge of our round border, and they flower at the most improbable times. Sometimes just when you might expect, simultaneously with the pink, lily-flowering *Tulipa* 'Jacqueline', but occasionally they also appear in October or March.

Trees for small gardens

Winter is the time when the actual structure of the garden becomes clearly visible. I will say more about this in January, but I now want to talk explicitly about trees. Far too often, the wrong tree is chosen for gardens of a limited size and after a few years it becomes much too big. But the damage has already been done. Therefore, it is extremely important to choose an appropriate tree that will not grow too tall for smaller gardens.

When our garden was laid out in 1985, previously planted trees already formed the basis. But it was still necessary to plant a few new trees to make the structure of the garden complete. The trees that were already there were a row of black birch trees (*Betula nigra*) and, at the other side of the garden, hawthorns (*Crataegus monogyna*). Hawthorns were planted on all fortifications in the Netherlands because of their defensive nature (prickly thorns!), and the birch trees were granted a place when there was a small nursery on the bastion for a short time back in the 1950s. The birch trees perform well as stately guardsmen at the main entrance to the garden and the hawthorns—thanks to premature intervention—are also well integrated into the garden. This type of tree grows naturally in a tangled, untidy fashion which matches the natural outer area of the dike but which was less suitable for the garden. And so we decided to prune the hawthorns in the shape of a parasol for our future garden, which brings them more into line with the character of the rest of the garden.

Betula nigra

Hawthorn (*Crataegus monogyna*) pruned to form a parasol

I was keen to add a few other, less-common trees that would eventually become a distinctive feature in the structure of the garden. They had to be trees that wouldn't grow too big so that they would not provide too much shade. I finally chose a three-stemmed *Magnolia obovata* (a big-leaf magnolia whose leaves are sometimes 45 cm long), a *Broussonetia papyrifera* (paper mulberry), and a *Prunus serrula* (Tibetan cherry). A *Cladrastis lutea* (yellow-wood) was planted just outside the garden proper, at the second entrance. The last three trees have grown to their full height of 6 m and form a roof over certain parts of the garden. The magnolia is even taller, at 10 m, but looks quite wispy because it is so slender. The nice thing is that, together, these trees display a succession of their best characteristics. The cherry has a magnificent trunk all year round: polished mahogany bark that peels away in bands to reveal terracotta strips, making it almost look as though ribbons have been tied around the tree. The paper

Halesia carolina Monticola Group

Cladrastis lutea

Magnolia obovata

mulberry has light green leaves that turn golden yellow in autumn and the same is true for the yellow-wood; this tree has an extra trump card in that it produces sweet-smelling, white catkins in June which resemble the flowers on wisteria. And finally, the magnolia, which as I mentioned has extremely large leaves, also produces large white flowers in May.

All of them are trees which would do well in an average private garden, as regards their size, just like the following species:

Acer capillipes (snake-bark maple)

Acer griseum (paperbark maple)

Amelanchier arborea 'Robin Hill' (Juneberry)

Amelanchier × *grandiflora* 'Ballerina' (snowy mespilus)

Cercis canadensis 'Forest Pansy' (redbud 'Forest Pansy')

Acer griseum   *Cercis canadensis* 'Forest Pansy'   *Prunus serrula*

Clerodendrum trichotomum var. *fargesii* (peanut butter tree, because if you rub the leaves, they smell of peanut butter)

Halesia carolina Monticola Group (mountain snowdrop tree)

Koelreuteria paniculata (pride of India)

Malus 'Evereste' (crab apple)

DREAM AWAY READING GARDEN BOOKS AND CATALOGUES

December is the best month to curl up by the fire with a pile of garden books and catalogues to dream about new plans and plants or read about the experiences of other garden enthusiasts. One of my first garden books—now falling apart because I have leafed through it so often—was *In Your Garden* by Vita Sackville-West. I even wrote the date in it: April 1980. It is lovely to see when I started studying plants in more depth. Vita Sackville-West describes what happens in her gardens at Sissinghurst every season throughout the year in this still-interesting and educational book.

Many other books have guided me to a greater or lesser extent in my attempts to learn more and more about planting and ways of managing it. My favourites are:

Dear Friend and Gardener: Letters on Life and Gardening by Beth Chatto and Christopher Lloyd
The Hillier Manual of Trees and Shrubs by John Hillier
The Education of a Gardener by Russell Page
Die Stauden und ihre Lebensbereiche (Perennials and Their Garden Habits) by Richard Hansen and Friedrich Stahl
Het Hessenhof Handboek, catalogue from De Hessenhof Perennial Plant Nursery, the Netherlands
The Dry Garden by Beth Chatto
Plantes pour Jardins Secs, catalogue from Pépinière Filippi, France
The Gardens of Gertrude Jekyll by Richard Bisgrove
Thompson & Morgan Seed Catalogue / Winter Catalogue

12 Months in My Garden

JANUARY

FEBRUARY

MAY

JUNE

SEPTEMBER

OCTOBER

MARCH

APRIL

JULY

AUGUST

NOVEMBER

DECEMBER

Anemone tomentosa 'Robustissima'

Favourite Plants: Pink

Pink is not my favourite colour, but if used in the right way, it can be a good addition. I use this colour very little in my own garden. On bright sunny days, pink quickly starts to look a bit grey. And so, if you are going to put pink into sunny borders, you need to make sure there are strong supporting colours nearby, such as purple, brown, ruby red, and dark green. Another possibility is to incorporate pink into matching colour shades such as white, violet, strawberry pink, and a splash of apricot: that way, the colours will merge into each other and then it's acceptable. If I ever do use pink, it is almost always in borders that are completely or partially in shadow. My top five pink plants for shady spots are:

Anisodontea capensis

Echinacea purpurea 'Fatal Attraction'

Erodium manescavii

Geranium sanguineum 'Apfelblüte'

Helleborus × ericsmithii 'Pirouette'

Hydrangea macrophylla 'Romance'

Lilium martagon

Papaver orientale 'Helen Elizabeth'

Lythrum virgatum 'Swirl'

JANUARY

The beginning of a new year is a good time to reflect. The excesses of December are followed by a quiet month and a feeling you can start afresh. It's a time when my hands itch to get going in the garden, but it is still a bit early. Snow and frost can easily undermine your efforts. And yet, in the distance, there is a glimmer of a new spring. The mild winters we've had recently often make it hard to resist the temptation. So I do go outside on days when it isn't too cold and make a start on removing seedlings from places I don't want them to grow, or I quickly transplant a few snowdrops which moles have pushed up out of the ground. My muscles always ache after that first day in the garden, but I'm happy to put up with that.

Sheep and Snowdrops

In 1985, I moved to Weesp: a new home and, in our case, a large new plot of land where all sorts of things were waiting to be discovered. The very first winter, hundreds of snowdrops suddenly appeared at the foot of large poplars under the dike. They were so lovely to see, because the plot had been badly neglected and that was the last thing I'd expected. The snowdrops finished and reappeared the following year and that went on for a few years until we decided to buy some Texel sheep to keep the grass on the dike under control. It became apparent that the sheep liked snowdrops too, because only a few appeared the following spring. Eventually, over the next few years, they disappeared completely. But sheep don't live forever either. When the last one died at a grand old age, we brought in new sheep, a dwarf variety this time: Ouessant sheep originally from the island of Ouessant off the coast of Brittany. These little sheep, with their French roots, are much fussier: they don't like eating snowdrops. Two years ago, to my great surprise, I saw the first little flowers appearing again in January. What probably happened was that the seeds of the first snowdrops recently started redeveloping into little bulbs capable of producing flowers, and they are now getting the chance to grow because the sheep leave them alone.

Field of snowdrops

Our Ouessant sheep amongst the snowdrops

The pond looks quite different in winter.

These snowdrops are the first signs of life in an otherwise bare plot. If I go for a walk around in January and look down from the dike, I notice all sorts of other things every year. One of them is our garden's structure. It is a structure you see most clearly when it is covered in a thin layer of snow.

Structure

Every garden needs a framework to create important and less important areas and to make the overall proportions visible. In our garden, this structure comprises trees, hedges, shrubs, and topiary. The trees are the first layer in the structure: they form the roof of the garden, so to speak, marking out the space above. The hedges are the second layer in the structure. Most of them are planted to frame the proper model garden. They form a green wall that says clearly, 'This is where one section stops and another, with a different function, begins'. It is a way of marking the boundary between the model garden and our private gardens. We have planted an oval hedge in the middle of the garden, surrounding an oval pond. That

hedge indicates the transition between two sections with different functions: a colourful garden on the outside and a tranquil spot on the inside with the pond as its only element. This hedge has furthermore been placed so strategically that you can't see the whole garden at once. And that also means that, when you wander through the garden, you have to go around the hedge and that is when you discover new things again and again.

The hedge in the centre of the garden is a *Thuja* hedge. It wasn't our first choice, but we were given it by a grower we know well which made it difficult to refuse. The hedge is now almost 40 years old. It hasn't always been kept tidy, because it's a huge job and I'm often too busy. That is why the hedge bulges here and there. You can't just cut out the bulges, though, because that would leave gaps. From that point of view, *Thuja* is not an easy species that recovers well. But, by pruning around the bulges, we have created an original, impressive shape: a stately element that provides a serene background to all the perennial borders around it.

When I laid out the garden, 40 years ago, I planted shrubs and topiaries in these perennial borders as the third layer in the structure. They are the connecting element between the various borders and provide a firm foundation for the whole garden. They form a framework that is particularly visible in the winter when the majority of the perennials have died back. The topiaries are largely clusters of box (*Buxus*) balls, alternating here and there with a bear or peacock shape which was in fashion at the time. I would not plant them nowadays, but there is something poignant about them. They act as supreme eye-catchers in the winter, adding allure to the almost bare garden, in expectation of new life. All sorts of things are happening underground and will eventually become visible when the first spring bulbs make their entrance.

In winter, frost does its bit to create structures in the garden.

Even more snowdrops (and other flowering species)

So let's return to the snowdrops, because being the very first flowers to bloom, they are invaluable. I'm not really a snowdrop collector—I only have four or five species—but I'm very attached to these little flowers as a sign of life in a new garden year.

Many years ago, I bought snowdrops in pots to cheer up a winter lunch by giving the table a festive look. They didn't last very long in the house though, and so before they completely withered away, I planted them outside in the garden around my house. They loyally appeared in larger and larger clumps every January. And then I found out that, to get them to multiply, it is actually better to replant them immediately after they have flowered. And so I set to work: carefully pulling the clumps apart and then putting them straight back into the ground as single plants or in twos and threes. This is called planting 'in the green', because they are transplanted in the period when they still have leaves. It is a very successful method, because now my garden is covered with a white blanket of hundreds of flowering snowdrops every January. They flower best in shady, slightly damp spots. If your soil is dry, you'll have to plant them about 8–10 cm deep.

Once the snowdrops are past their peak, the spring snowflakes (*Leucojum vernum*) start to flower. I have three clumps of them in my garden which I got from Piet Oudolf ages ago. I was walking around his garden with him one winter's day when I spotted a group of these little plants, not quite in flower, in a shady spot at the back of his farmhouse. When I asked what they were, he couldn't immediately tell me, but he said, 'Take a few if you like.' I went home with a ball of earth I'd dug up, and every time they flower, I think of their generous donor. They are doing well but have not really spread. That confirms what I've read about *Leucojum vernum*: 'A difficult species, which definitely needs to be kept cool and damp. Only spreads in ideal conditions.'

Leucojum vernum

The first signs of spring can be seen even in January.

But not everything that flowers in this period is small and modest. Our *Viburnum × bodnantense* 'Dawn', a 40-year-old shrub we've had from the very beginning, produces pale pink, sweet-scented clusters of flowers from as early as November. At 4 m high and almost as wide, it is impressive to behold. It is in a spot I pass every day, and so I can regularly enjoy it in this period too. Over the years, I have stripped the main stems from the bottom to prevent the viburnum from becoming a heavy, dominating shrub. The disadvantage is that suckers start to grow as soon as you start to prune it. Suckers are fast-growing branches that emerge when a tree or shrub suddenly needs to restore its leaf surface area after it has been pruned. But if you remove the sucker in the middle of the summer, there will be little chance to repeat the regrowth. That is the way to keep the shrub's shape under control. It will continue to flower until well into March, although this viburnum will keep itself in check in cold periods and then flower happily again when the temperature rises.

Inspiration

The summer brings an oversupply of inspiration, generated by gardens open to the public, parks, nurseries, and plant fairs. There is never enough time to see everything. But there is none of that in the winter, and you need to rely on other forms of inspiration. I find inspiration in exhibitions,

Liège Station designed by the architect Santiago Calatrava

Amsterdam Light Festival

Colourful display in the market

Pedestrian footbridge in Antwerp

but it can also be found in changes outdoors such as new buildings, bridges, street furniture, and art forms in outdoor spaces, such as the Amsterdam Light Festival. Another thing that makes me very happy is when I see beauty somewhere I least expect it: at a market, for example, where a creative stallholder has set out his produce like a work of art.

GARDEN TOOLS

I read an article by Romke van de Kaa, a famous Dutch garden writer, in which he expressed surprise at the enormous number of garden tools some garden enthusiasts have. In that context, he wrote, 'How many of us need a dandelion weeder or an asparagus cutter?' The first one especially hit home because my 'dandelion weeder' has often served me well: when digging

out sorrel, for instance, or when planting bulbs that will naturalise in grass. The latter is no easy task, because you have to stab through the turf, and a dandelion weeder makes your job much easier! Otherwise, my collection of tools is quite modest; apart from the duplicates (handy if you lose one), I have twelve different implements:

lawn rake	wheelbarrow
bulb planter	weeding fork
dandelion weeder	small grass hook
watering can	trowels, various sizes and shapes
hedge trimmer	secateurs
scraper	spade

Almost all the small tools have wooden handles. I have painted them orange because it is so irritating if you put your trowel to one side for a moment when you're working and then can't find it again. February is the time to take them all out of hibernation, and I can't wait!

12 Months in My Garden

JANUARY

FEBRUARY

MAY

JUNE

SEPTEMBER

OCTOBER

MARCH

APRIL

JULY

AUGUST

NOVEMBER

DECEMBER

Favourite Plants: White

White is a lovely colour because it is so neutral and because you can use white in numerous combinations. White is sometimes literally 'light in darkness' because white flowers shine like lights in dark spots and make everything brighter. White honesty, columbine, *Cimicifuga*, *Geranium*, *Aster divaricatus*, and *Campanula* are just a few examples. White is almost dazzling in the sun: something that always sparkles in between all the other colours. It is ideal as a way of combining mixed groups of plants; *Gaura lindheimeri* 'Whirling Butterflies' is one of my favourites, as is *Anemone × hybrida* 'Honorine Jobert'. But plenty of perennials will be discussed in various other chapters. So for now I will give you a list of my favourite shrubs, two trees, a climbing plant, and—in spite of what I just said—two perennials:

Lavatera 'White Angel'

Amelanchier lamarckii

Choisya × *dewitteana* 'Aztec Pearl'

Clematis 'Paul Farges'

Clerodendrum trichotomum
var. *fargesii*

Exochorda × *macrantha* 'The Bride'

Hydrangea macrophylla 'Madame Emile
Mouillère'

Magnolia obovata

Romneya coulteri

Viburnum plicatum 'Watanabe'

FEBRUARY

February is a treacherous and dangerous month, the most unre-
liable of them all. Some years it still has days with a hard frost
and the next year everything goes so fast that you want to get
going as soon as you can. I like structure and planning. February
is a disaster in that respect, because you can't plan anything. My
strategy is just to play it by ear from one year to the next and go
into the garden as soon as the sun shines and the temperature
is above zero. The knowledge that it won't be long until spring
bursts into colour is also a good reason to persevere.

Prune, Rake, and Tidy Up

There is nothing I like better than to get my wheelbarrow out on a sunny day in February, gather all the other tools, and get to work. I start in the most sheltered borders that get the sun, where everything starts sprouting soonest. I cut back all the perennials and ornamental grasses, except for those species susceptible to frost such as *Gaura* and lavender—they need to wait until March. Shrubs are reshaped where necessary or even cut right back, because they will then produce the most flowers; the same applies to the profusely flowering St John's wort (*Hypericum* × *inodorum* 'Elstead'). But I leave the hydrangeas for now. They still look quite decorative with their dried flowers, and if you cut them off there is a greater risk of frost damage.

Hypericum × inodorum 'Elstead' after pruning

Decorative dried hydrangea flowers

Pollarding willows with the girls from next door

Golden wood millet seedlings

Once most of the pruning has been done, it is time to do some weeding. It is amazing how early in the season these unwanted plants become established in the borders: ash seedlings from the trees a bit further away on our land whose tiny grey stems and black buds give them away in the bare borders. But also sneaky young sorrel plants, the bright yellow leaves of golden wood millet (*Milium effusum* 'Aureum'), and the dark green little hairy bittercress (*Cardamine hirsuta*). Yes, I know that bittercress contains a lot of vitamin C in its green basal rosettes, that they taste peppery, and that you can eat them in salads, but I would rather be rid of them because, as soon as they flower, they disperse dozens of seeds.

And then there is the question of fallen leaves: Should you rake them out of the borders when tidying up or leave them be? I favour the latter to prevent the soil from drying out and deteriorating in quality. But not far from the corner of the garden, we have an enormous beech tree which drops masses of leaves (and beech nuts) in autumn and winter. If I don't rake them up, thick clods of leaves will stick together which do not decompose easily. I remove as much of them as possible after the winter. They have protected the plants in the coldest period, but if I leave them in the spring the plants suffocate. The only remedy is to carefully rake the leaves up—quite a job.

Iris 'Katherine Hodgkin'

Hellebores in an early-spring border

Discovery and inspiration

On days like these, I sometimes crawl on hands and knees through the garden to get at everything. Occasionally, I feel like an explorer in my own garden. You constantly come across new surprises as you tidy up. That happens every year of course, but it still gives you a great burst of energy each time you see close up how your garden is doing its best to come to life again: the crimson buds of the peonies, the first grey-green tips of *Iris* 'Katherine Hodgkin' which flower within a week, and the countless seedlings you get to know at such an early stage.

Often I feel less tired after a long day working in the garden than after spending a day sitting at my desk, working on my computer or at my drawing board. The garden literally gives you adrenalin and helps you to clear your head again. As you prune, weed, and rake, you can let your thoughts roam, and often, after a day's work outdoors, I come up with the solution to a problem I've been wrestling with indoors, at my desk.

Self-seeders

The other things I encounter in large numbers as I walk around the garden are the self-seeders: plants which hold their own by spreading seeds and which you come across in all sorts of different places. Whole colonies of

Smyrnium amongst the gravel

Helleborus orientalis seedlings

Papaver somniferum 'Lauren's Grape' in sunnier spots

Smyrnium, Lunaria rediviva (perennial honesty), *Digitalis lutea* (small yellow foxglove), *Aquilegia* (columbine), and *Helleborus orientalis* and *H. foetidus* (Christmas rose and stinking hellebore) emerge in damper spots. In drier spots, and particularly at the edge of our gravel paths, I always find seedlings of *Verbascum blattaria* (moth mullein), *Linaria* (toadflax), *Myosotis* (forget-me-not), *Erysimum* (wallflower), *Verbena bonariensis* (Argentinian vervain), *Milium*, and *Erigeron karvinskianus* (Mexican fleabane). *Papaver cambricum* (Welsh poppy) and *Primula elatior* (oxlip) spread all over the garden, regardless of whether the spot is sunny or shady, dry, or quite damp.

The oxlip especially cloaks the garden in sulphur-yellow in March and April. I go round the borders many times in those months to dig out a clump here and there for visitors who dearly want to grow this plant too. Once this oxlip and the Welsh poppy establish themselves in your garden, you'll never get rid of them, but I rather like their modesty and delicate colours.

The most unpredictable of the self-seeders is a poppy I once bought as a seed at a garden in Zeeland. Obviously, I planted it in the hottest and sunniest border in relatively dry soil, but it took me quite a while before I found out how to get it to flower every year. Poppies like turned-over soil, which means you have to use a trowel to dig over the spot every year. The soil gets disturbed, but it does create ideal conditions for poppies. They tend to be more prominent in some years than others and they don't

Helleborus × *ericsmithii* 'Pirouette' appears as early as February.

flower for long, but the colour is fantastic: deep purple. I bought them unlabelled, but they are probably *Papaver somniferum* 'Lauren's Grape'.

Renovation

You don't really notice subtle changes when you walk past the same plants in your garden every day, but when I saw photos of my garden 30 years ago, in 1985, I could clearly see that what had been relatively young trees then have since grown into enormous specimens. When we had a summer storm in July 2017 and lost a few willows and ash trees, it was time to get someone in to look seriously at all the trees and assess their health and life expectancy.

We got a firm of tree specialists to draw up a report and it emerged that various trees had come to the end of their lives and that some were even seriously diseased. That last group included three black birch trees to the

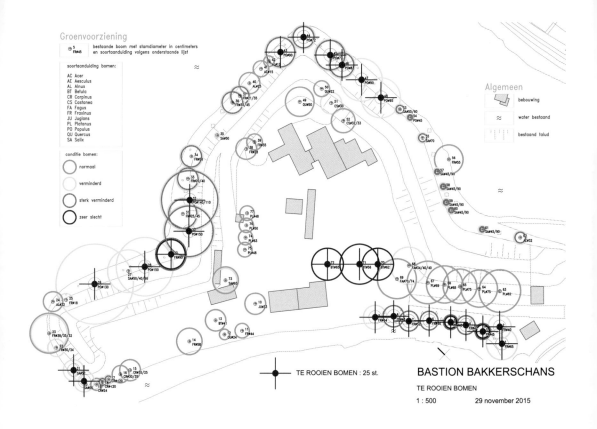

TE ROOIEN BOMEN : 25 st.

BASTION BAKKERSCHANS

TE ROOIEN BOMEN

1 : 500   29 november 2015

Report on the health of the trees in our garden. The red symbols show which trees have come to the end of their lives and have to be dug up. It's time for something new.

south of the model garden. They had been attacked by honey fungus to a greater or lesser extent and so, one fine day in February, they were sawn down. We were sad to see them go and the new look of the garden took some time getting used to, but the huge amount of light that now comes in is fantastic. And it opened up opportunities for giving the borders that had been in the shadow of these great trees a good facelift. The first plants to benefit from all the new light were the crocuses (*Crocus chrysanthus* 'Gipsy Girl'). Before, they had only opened later in the afternoon, once the last rays of sun reached them, but now, on a clear day, they stand up straight and their flowers are wide open from about noon.

Precautionary measures

Now that we are talking about spring-flowering bulbs: February is also the month to start thinking about your tulips. I always try to garden as sustainably as possible, and one of the resolutions I made over 20 years ago when I started working with spring-flowering bulbs was never to remove the bulbs from the ground after they had flowered. The same applies to tulips. In all those years I have learned how to ensure that they last as long as possible and flower every year, even if the blooms are slightly smaller. One of the measures I take is to scatter cow dung pellets in between them when they first poke their noses out of the ground in February. These organic granules release their active substances over a period of 2 to 3 months, and that means that this additional nutrition is available for the tulips right at the moment they need it most: immediately after they have flowered, when they need to gather their strength again to make a new bulb that will flower the following year. The result is that some cultivated varieties in my garden such as *Tulipa* 'Orange Emperor', 'Recreado', and 'White Triumphator' have been coming back for 10 to 15 years.

Tulips start poking their
heads up this month.

12 Months in My Garden

JANUARY

FEBRUARY

MAY

JUNE

SEPTEMBER

OCTOBER

MARCH

APRIL

JULY

AUGUST

NOVEMBER

DECEMBER

Allium nigrum

Favourite Plants: Plants with Structure

Some plants have a sort of second life. They are not only beautiful when flowering, but before or after flowering they also have special characteristics which make them attractive for a longer period. One of these characteristics is their structure after flowering: a clear-cut, graphic image that makes these types of plants worth looking at even in the winter.

Aconitum carmichaelii 'Arendsii'

Calamagrostis × acutiflora 'Overdam'

Hakonechloa macra

Hydrangea aspera 'Macrophylla'

Hydrangea macrophylla

Hypericum × inodorum 'Elstead'

Lunaria rediviva

Nassella tenuissima

Verbena bonariensis

MARCH

March is the month I always look forward to. Officially, March 1 is the first day of the meteorological spring, but apart from that, everything around you just makes you aware that nature is holding its breath and waiting for the right moment to explode with colour. I can remember days in March when I stood in the snow, filling pots with forced bulbs as part of my work at the Keukenhof Gardens. But equally, there could be days when I was working outside in a T-shirt, enjoying the spring sunshine and temperatures of around 20°C (68°F). March is all of that; it is a month full of surprises.

The Force of Nature

Most of the early work in the garden was done in February, and so March does not bring an abundance of garden activities, apart from a few jobs that absolutely have to be done in this period. But March is a month which lends itself to philosophising about how you really view your garden. When we made this model garden in 1985, the idea was to show visitors what our ideal garden would look like: a garden with an emphasis on plant arrangements in the various borders, with different biotopes and in a more or less natural setting. I kept to this as much as possible, but apart from the fact that it is always nice to have a beautiful garden, it has also become clear to me over the years that this garden means much more to me than that. It is also my lifeblood, because I couldn't live without a garden–and particularly this garden.

When I'm working outside, I almost feel sorry for visitors who ask me if it isn't an awful lot of work to maintain this garden. They don't realise that I derive a huge amount of energy from it, as well as essential inspiration for my work. The garden and I live in a sort of symbiosis. I look after the garden and constantly make decisions in pursuit of an ideal. And the

garden responds—sometimes in very surprising ways—and that again is the power of nature.

Now that I am writing this book and looking at my garden through the lens of a camera many times every month, to record as much as I can, I notice that I am seeing the garden differently too. As I put certain angles into a frame, I see things that would otherwise have passed me by. Imperfections become visible more quickly, but equally often, it is lovely to see that the image is just right. It is and remains a learning process. And that puts me in mind of what Edward Flint, head gardener of a private estate in England, once said in an interview, 'Your eyes are your most important tools; use them, be critical: stop, look, think.' That really appeals to me.

Tulipa praestans 'Shogun' in a pot

Mini gardens

After this philosophical digression, sleeves still have to be rolled up again because March is the ideal month for mini gardens. That means filling pots with seasonal plants, including spring-flowering bulbs, which are also known as 'forced' bulbs. When the first little pots

Arrangement of different species of grape hyacinth with pansies and branches of dragon's claw willow

of 'Tête-à-Tête' daffodils appear in our local supermarket, I long to buy them. But if you look a bit further afield, you will find an exuberance of more unusual ready-planted bulbs in flower shops, garden centres, and at market stalls. And then there's nothing better than to plant these spring-flowering bulbs in pots together with forget-me-nots, *Bellis*, pansies, wallflowers, and small shrubs such as *Skimmia* and *Viburnum tinus*. Sometimes I also stick a few sprigs of red dogwood, cornelian cherry, or weeping willow in amongst them, since they add just a bit more volume. These kinds of pots are ideal for making the garden look attractive in this rather bare phase. So I place them near the entrance to the garden, next to a bench, or against the fence around our private garden: small touches which have a major effect.

Back when I was making plans for the Keukenhof Gardens, between 2004 and 2012, and I was helping to make various corners look attractive in the last two weeks before the opening, I learned to indulge myself by combining forced spring-flowering bulbs with other early-flowering garden plants. Every spring, in the run-up to the opening, we made a fixed basis of little shrubs, ornamental grasses, and spring-flowering plants, and then planted bulbs grown in pots in between them which were then replaced as soon as they had finished flowering. That gives you a pot that

Arrangements of spring-flowering bulbs in pots put together for the Keukenhof Gardens

always looks its best from mid-March to the second half of May, something which is easy to copy for your own garden. And then, at the end of May, you fill the same pot with summer flowers.

The only thing you need is a reasonably sized pot, at least 25 cm in diameter and 25 cm in height. If you use smaller pots, there is a risk of the plants drying out and the fixed basis will be unable to develop properly. Fill the pots with a mixture of good potting compost and sand in the ratio 4:1. A mixture of this kind ensures that excess water drains away quickly.

Ingredients for a pretty spring arrangement in a pot: white multiflora hyacinths, white grape hyacinths, and orange pansies, with twigs of red dogwood to give it some height

And finally, arrange the plants in the pots, press the soil down well, and give the whole lot its first good drink of water. You will have to continue watering the plants in the pots regularly, because plants above the ground dry out much more quickly than plants which grow in the ground.

Pruning and replanting

That is not the end of the work which needs to be done in March, because there are still some shrubs, perennials, and climbing plants which have to be dealt with one last time before they are ready for the new season. This is the month in which I snip off the old flowers from the hydrangeas, cut back the lavender and *Gaura* even further, and use my sharp scissors on my clematis.

Almost all clematis in our garden hold onto trees or shrubs, and so I only have to guide them in the direction of the nearest supports if they look untidy. They will then find their own way and grasp onto their host's branches. They flower at different times in the summer, but in March I prune them all back to the first pair of sturdy buds, which are usually about 50 to 100 cm above the ground. There is one exception: a species which produces abundant white flowers at the end of May. It has worked its way up through the hawthorns which happen to flower at the same

The clematis that has entwined itself in the hawthorn

Cutting off old hydrangea flowers

time on the inner side of the dike. It has become such a tyrant that I will never be able to get it out of the bushes again, but it seems happy so far so I leave it be. Unfortunately, I can't tell you its name, so I'll just have to wait until a visitor arrives who is knowledgeable about clematis.

And of course, we still had to plant new trees to replace the black birch trees which departed this life last month. That could just be done in March, and so we finally chose two species whose scale matches the size of the garden somewhat better than the birch trees that had to go. *Styphnolobium japonicum* 'Regent' is a species of tree that has the same transparent look in its crown as the birch—because now I have so much more light, I didn't want to lose it straight away. This Japanese pagoda tree grows to a maximum height of about 12 m and will be the new eye-catcher in the southern border. If all goes well, it should produce large groups of creamy white flowers in 6 years' time, making it a good source of food for bees. A second species of tree that was planted in the same border is *Koelreuteria paniculata*, the golden rain tree. Instead of choosing one with a straight trunk and a crown on top, we went for a multi-stemmed, spiky bush shape. It only grows to a height of roughly 7 m which makes it the link between the 'roof' of this border and the shorter plants in it.

Digging the holes took a lot of effort. There were all sorts of roots from the dead birch trees in the ground. Furthermore, the soil in this border

Narcissus 'February Gold'

Dwarf daffodil *Narcissus* 'Little Gem'

Scilla mischtschenkoana

Scilla siberica

appearing everywhere, and the almost luminous tufts of *Milium effusum* 'Aureum' are getting bigger every day.

Long live spring, you might think, it's all starting. But what a disappointment when the weather vane suddenly turns towards the northeast again and a cold wind blows. A wind that ushers in dark clouds bringing thick snowflakes on a day that started so promisingly clear. March is showing its changeable side once more. And yet, I'm still optimistic, because there is a wonderful saying: 'Springtime is the land awakening, and the March winds are the morning yawn.'

12 Months in My Garden

JANUARY

FEBRUARY

MAY

JUNE

SEPTEMBER

OCTOBER

MARCH

APRIL

JULY

AUGUST

NOVEMBER

DECEMBER

Agapanthus 'Blue Heaven'

Favourite Plants: Sky-Blue

Throughout the rest of the year, you will rarely see a sky as clear and blue as it is in March. And that is why sky-blue is exactly the right colour for March, also because there are many spring-flowering bulbous plants in this colour. By logical extension, the list that follows partly contains spring-flowering bulbs, but I cannot resist listing some other plants too—annuals, orangery plants, biennials, and perennials, all of which are an improbable blue:

Amsonia orientalis

Anemone blanda 'Blue Shades'

Cichorium intybus

Dianella tasmanica

Hyacinthoides hispanica

Ipomoea tricolor 'Heavenly Blue'

Myosotis sylvatica

Omphalodes nitida

Salvia uliginosa

RIBBONS OF BULBS, KEUKENHOF GARDENS

In the years when I drew up plans for the Keukenhof Gardens, between 2004 and 2012, one element I found hugely enjoyable to work on was the ribbons of bulbs. A series of fourteen parallel borders, all 1.60 m wide but of varying lengths, displayed a different mixture of spring-flowering bulbs every year. The underlying idea was that they could act as examples of borders for public green spaces but wouldn't be out of place in private gardens either. I've selected two of these borders to show you here as an example, and I will explain a bit about them.

An early-flowering shrub, such as *Exochorda* (pearl bush, producing white flowers in April and May), always formed the basis. The rest of the borders were planted with spring-flowering bulbs, ensuring there would be colour from early in the season (end of March) to late (mid-May). That involved planting in two layers: early-flowering bulbs on the top and later-flowering ones below. If we take border 1 as an example, a mixture of tulips and daffodils would have been planted randomly in the lower layer with a mixture of *Puschkinia*, *Chionodoxa*, *Muscari*, and the two species of hyacinths planted haphazardly on the upper layer. In border 2, once again, the tulips and daffodils would have been planted in the lower layer, and *Anemone*, *Muscari*, and hyacinths planted in the upper layer. In practice, that means first planting the lower layer about 15 cm deep, and then the upper layer about 7 cm deep.

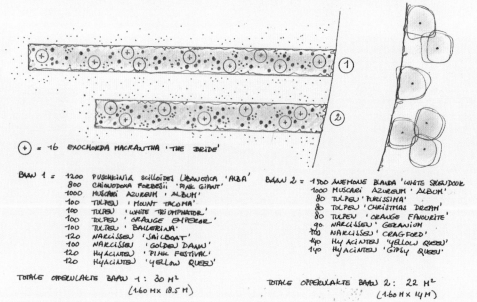

⊕ = 16 EXOCHORDA MACRANTHA 'THE BRIDE'

BAAN 1 =
1200	PUSCHKINIA SCILLOIDES LIBANOTICA 'ALBA'
800	CHIONODOXA FORBESII 'PINK GIANT'
1000	MUSCARI AZUREUM 'ALBUM'
100	TULPEN 'MOUNT TACOMA'
100	TULPEN 'WHITE TRIUMPHATOR'
100	TULPEN 'ORANGE EMPEROR'
100	TULPEN 'BALLERINA'
120	NARCISSEN 'SAILBOAT'
100	NARCISSEN 'GOLDEN DAWN'
120	HYACINTEN 'PINK FESTIVAL'
120	HYACINTEN 'YELLOW QUEEN'

BAAN 2 =
1500	ANEMONE BLANDA 'WHITE SPLENDOUR'
1000	MUSCARI AZUREUM 'ALBUM'
80	TULPEN 'PURISSIMA'
80	TULPEN 'CHRISTMAS DREAM'
80	TULPEN 'ORANGE FAVOURITE'
90	NARCISSEN 'GERANIUM'
100	NARCISSEN 'CRAGFORD'
140	HYACINTEN 'YELLOW QUEEN'
140	HYACINTEN 'GIPSY QUEEN'

TOTALE OPPERVLAKTE BAAN 1: 30 M²
(1.60 M X 18.5 M)

TOTALE OPPERVLAKTE BAAN 2: 22 M²
(1.60 M X 14 M)

APRIL

April is without a doubt the most uplifting of all the months. Growth in the garden suddenly seems to gain momentum and the ripple of progress in March—when the garden's gradual development was clear to see from day to day—turns into a cascade of new discoveries every day. And not just one, but several at a time until I feel I can't take it all in. The whole garden is joyfully shouting 'spring', and as a result I suddenly seem to have much more energy too.

Bulbs, Bulbs, and Yet More Bulbs

Spring-flowering bulbs are mainly what set the tone in this early period. Because we have different areas in our garden with their own biotopes, I can choose from a huge number of different species and there is almost no spring-flowering bulb which does not feature in our garden. Even hyacinths—those pompous, seemingly unnatural monsters, in my view, which fall over at the slightest suggestion of bad weather—have been granted a place. But they date back to the time when I had just started planting bulbs and wanted to try everything. And so a corner was planted with 'Delft Blue' hyacinths. But because I leave all the bulbs in the ground after they have flowered, they have become much less massive (and so more refined). Now they are short, sturdy clusters which spread a heavenly scent in the first week of April ... and so they may stay!

Even in the darkest, wettest border, at the foot of the dike, different species come and go: mainly daffodils such as 'February Silver', 'Jenny', 'Sailboat', and 'Ice Wings' which have faithfully continued to return for many years, but also *Leucojum aestivum* 'Gravetye Giant' (summer snowflake), which feels at home in these damp conditions. One plant I really regret planting ages ago is *Allium ursinum* (wild garlic). It has sweet little white flowers and pale green leaves that can be used to make a delicious pesto, but what vigour it has and what an ability to proliferate! Add to that its tendency to spread everywhere, especially in places you don't want it

Narcissus 'Jenny'

Leucojum aestivum 'Gravetye Giant'

Tulipa 'Orange Princess', *Tulipa turkestanica*, and *Tulipa* 'Lady Jane'

Tulipa 'White Triumphator' and 'Black Hero'

Tulipa 'Jewel of Spring', *Tulipa* 'Ballerina', and *Tulipa praestans* 'Shogun'

Tulipa 'Daydream', 'Ballerina', and 'West Point'

The seedlings of grape hyacinths and forget-me-nots popping up between the tiles look so nice that I just leave them there.

Tulipa 'Jacqueline' and 'Mariette'

Tulipa 'Spring Green', 'West Point', and 'Ballerina'

to be. I found this out too late: this plant belongs in damp woods where it can do what it wants, but not in a private garden!

Tulips set the trend in sunnier, drier spots. They are amongst my favourite spring-flowering bulbs because they are so prominent and yet elegantly present. There are so many different shapes and colours of flowers, heights, and flowering times that it has become a game for me to keep coming up with new combinations. That doesn't really apply in my own garden because most of the tulips have been there for years, but I enjoy doing this profusely in all sorts of other projects. If the occasional tulip in my garden perishes, I have no regrets at all, because it means I have the chance to try out a new, complementary cultivar again.

In the warmest and lightest spot, I grow a combination of cultivars in yellow, orange, and almost red which have done well there for years. The basis is provided by *Tulipa* 'Apricot Beauty', *Tulipa* 'Ballerina', and *Tulipa orphanidea* (a dwarf botanic species) in shades of orange; *Tulipa* 'West Point' and 'Flashback' in yellow; *Tulipa* 'Daydream' which changes colour from bright yellow to warm orange while flowering; and *Tulipa* 'Request' and 'Recreado' which provide a darker note in terracotta and rich purple, respectively. *Tulipa* 'Request' is my most recent acquisition, and we'll have to wait and see how dependable it is. But it certainly takes the combination to an even higher level.

Tulips have to be deadheaded after they have flowered. This enables them to retain enough strength to flower again next year.

Shades of pink dominate in the adjacent round border where two lily-flowered tulips, *Tulipa* 'Jacqueline' (not called after me) and 'Mariette', take the leading role around the edge. They are almost identical but differ in height: 'Jacqueline' grows to a height of 60 cm, while 'Mariette' only just reaches a height of 45 cm, but it is exactly that difference in height that gives them a gentler look.

At a certain point, an imposing, bright red tulip with a large, cup-shaped flower appeared in this pink edge. I had probably found a single bulb somewhere in the garden the previous autumn and, thinking it was a 'Jacqueline' or a 'Mariette', planted it in the round border. But this alien looked awful and was also demanding considerable attention. The only remedy was to snip off the flower, cut off all the leaves down to the ground, and hope it would give up. But to my surprise, two more red tulip flowers appeared the following spring ... *grrrr*, let's see who will win this battle! I tried to dig the intruder out that spring, but it wasn't so easy because there was a paper mulberry shrub with surface roots in the same bed. I anxiously awaited developments the following spring. To my utter surprise, this time a small bouquet of red tulips developed, and now I am the one who has given up. If I find them very annoying, I snip off the flowers, but other-wise I just leave them be. It's a good story in any case.

It's time to deadhead when the flowers stay open in the evening.

It's a story that isn't really consistent with the characteristics assigned to tulips, because they are reputed to be 'difficult'. While you can leave all the other spring-flowering bulbs to get on with growing, flowering, and then dying off, tulips—as befits a true diva—need some care. Incidentally, that does not apply to botanic tulips, because they can look after them-selves. But it does apply to the long-stemmed, more cultivated species, and that care consists of deadheading the flowers. Once they have finished flowering, when the petals stop folding in the evening and the flower stays open, this flower must be cut off as high up the stem as possible. Keep the remaining stem and the leaves because they need to catch as much light as possible to start the photosynthesis process: under the influence of that light, carbon dioxide in the plant is converted into sugar, which then pro-duces food for next year's new bulb.

The Flower Bulb Festival

After spending years planting bulbs until I felt that hardly any more would fit, my garden eventually looked so gorgeous one April about 10 years ago that I thought it would be a shame not to organise a special bulb

Tulipa 'Jacqueline' and 'Mariette' add splashes of colour in amongst the green.

Tulipa 'Yellow Purissima', 'Jewel of Spring', 'White Triumphator', and 'Aladdin'

weekend in that period. And that was the start of our Flower Bulb Festival, which now attracts garden enthusiasts and garden clubs from the Netherlands and abroad. During the third weekend of April, our garden becomes the centre of attention for three consecutive days. The bulbs and how they are combined with burgeoning perennials are what it's all about, of course. But to give visitors an opportunity to take something of the atmosphere back home, there is also a small market selling ready-planted bulbs and unusual perennials and biennials.

Organising an event of this kind is one thing, but the weather is quite another. Usually we're lucky, but 3 years ago we had such a cold spring that there was hardly anything to see in that third weekend in April. Well, 'February Gold' and 'W.P. Milner' daffodils were in flower and the first scillas were making a hesitant appearance, but that was about it. There was no sign of tulips at all and that was unfortunate for the foreign visitors. For 3 days I did little else than explain that nature won't be forced. Eventually, people were very understanding, luckily. It was also freezing cold, so spending a lot of time outside wasn't exactly fun. But the warmth of the wood-burning stove in the Tea House amply made up for it, and the following year, thanks to an extremely hot spring, when everything flowered profusely and simultaneously, the disaster of the previous year was soon forgotten.

Planting bulbs at Keukenhof Gardens

Keukenhof Gardens are always on my list of gardens to visit in the spring. I don't find the layout very spectacular, but it is the perfect place to brush up your knowledge of bulbs and to gaze in admiration at new species and cultivars. And nowadays I have a rather emotional connection with them. You see, back in 2003, I was asked to renovate a section of the park. One of the oldest sections, known as Smalle Bos—first planted over 50 years ago—was now almost overcrowded and was in urgent need of renovation. The executive director at the time, Jan Willem Wessel, was a forward-thinking man with vision. He had the idea of looking at Keukenhof Gardens from a different angle: in addition to the fairly conservative layout of the main part of the park, which was all about bulbs and little else, he wanted to create a place where visitors could see what they could do with bulbs in their own gardens, in combination with other plants. And the former Smalle Bos was the obvious spot.

I heard about the project through the grapevine, and I was asked whether I would consider taking it on. A dream project! The keywords for the new layout were *innovation, inspiration*, and *education*; with those

Ribbons of tulips designed for the Keukenhof Gardens

Bridal Avenue designed for the Keukenhof Gardens with *Ajuga reptans* 'Catlin's Giant', *Brunnera macrophylla* 'Variegata', and *Omphalodes verna* forming the basis, interspersed by *Tulipa* 'Purissima', *Tulipa* 'Apricot Beauty', *Tulipa* 'Apricot Impression', and *Narcissus* 'Sailboat'

concepts at the back of my mind, I set to work. The new design contained all sorts of elements which were not only intended to give private visitors new ideas, but also the people working in public green spaces. The end result was a merging of shrubs, perennials, biennial spring flowers, and spring-flowering bulbs placed in seven Inspirational Gardens, a field of Flower Ribbons, a Bridal Avenue, a Spring Meadow, and a corner with pansy hills, where a wide range of spring pansies were combined with bulbous plants. The most enjoyable part of this project was that I didn't need to stop once the drawings were finished; I also became intensively involved in planning and laying out the 2.5-ha area. The new section was officially opened in March 2005 by Princess Margriet of the Netherlands, whom I accompanied on a walk around the park. I visited the park at least twice a week that same spring to see how everything was growing and what the public's reactions were.

They were, to put it mildly, divided. Older, regular visitors, who valued Keukenhof Gardens for their regimented beds in which red tulips, yellow daffodils, and blue hyacinths vied for attention, did not like it at all: too messy, too many other plants demanding attention, and too many intermingled colours. But younger people reacted enthusiastically; they gained new ideas in the Inspiration Gardens and saw with their own eyes how easy it is to put a pot of spring plants together. Fortunately, the flock of fans grew steadily in the following years, and Keukenhof Gardens received compliments from all sides for its new approach. And yet the idyll came to an end after spring 2011—a new executive director and a new park manager was one of the reasons. And so gradually the old dogma resurfaced: Keukenhof Gardens' purpose is to present bulbs, and everything unconnected with that is too much unnecessary ballast. Shame, shame, shame!

Planting bulbs at the neighbours'

One of my first large-scale bulb projects abroad, in Germany in this case, crossed my path as a consequence of the World's Fair Expo 2000 in Hannover. I had made the planting plan for the garden around the Dutch pavilion, which was designed to resemble landscapes stacked on top of each other from an idea by MVRDV, a firm of architects. My garden included masses of perennials, annuals, and summer-flowering bulbs which surrounded the building like a vast flower meadow. From the end of May until October, the constant alternation of colours and heights made a big impression on many visitors. One of them was Baroness Viktoria von dem Bussche, the owner of a castle in Bad Essen, near Osnabrück. She soon approached me and asked if I would come and take a look at her garden— actually a park of several hectares. As a result, I have done something there

Designs for spring planting for Schloss Ippenburg, where bulbs played a major role

every year since 2002: mainly using spring-flowering bulbs, but sometimes also perennials and annuals.

The high point came when Bad Essen was chosen to host the National Garden Festival in 2010. The baroness grabbed the opportunity to make radical changes, and I was commissioned to come up with a new plant scheme for a variety of places in the park. These garden festivals always run from April until October, so several ingredients were introduced: perennials, hundreds of spring-flowering bulbs, summer-flowering annuals, and summer-flowering bulbs. That meant that plans had to be made in 2009. All the plants were planted in November, with the help of a few gardener friends, and again in May, when the spring-flowering bulbs had to be exchanged for summer-flowering bulbs and annuals. It was great fun and felt literally like a party, especially when everything was in flower and radiating exuberance. Everyone was happy!

Early-flowering perennials

When the slim oxlips (*Primula elatior*) come into flower in March and April and roll out a pale lemon blanket over the garden, for a while it seems as if they are the only ones flowering so early. But that is deceptive, because if you look closely you will see other shades of lemon and chartreuse-yellow here and there, alternating with white and a little powder blue.

The plant that unquestionably deserves the most admiration in April is *Cardamine heptaphylla*, a sort of giant cuckoo flower with white flowers and much-divided leaves. I first saw it years ago in a woodland garden in England, and I was immediately captivated by it. I took a cutting back to Weesp. It was a while before it got going, but since then I have divided the original plant into several pieces, and it is now flaunting itself in various shady places.

The yellow spring border with tulips and primulas

The giant cuckoo flower (*Cardamine heptaphylla*)

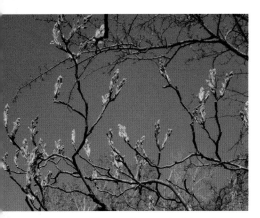

The Juneberry in bud (*Amelanchier lamarckii*)

A plant whose flower is very similar is *Lunaria rediviva* (perennial honesty), which flowers a little later, grows a bit taller, and has completely different toothed, triangular, heart-shaped leaves. Seed capsules form after flowering; later in the year, after the seeds have fallen out, they change into silver-white medallions which look attractive almost all winter. *Lunaria rediviva* is another good plant for dark corners, but it does spread rather vigorously, forming seedlings with such a strong taproot that they are almost impossible to remove.

The chartreuse-yellow flowers are mainly *Euphorbia* which start flowering in April: *Euphorbia amygdaloides* var. *robbiae*, *Euphorbia characias* subsp. *wulfenii*, *Euphorbia polychroma*, and *Euphorbia griffithii* 'Fireglow' with orange flowers. And then there is *Milium effusum* 'Aureum' (Bowles's golden grass) which is now showing its luminous leaves to the full. The delicate blue comes from the flowers of the various *Brunnera* species: *Brunnera macrophylla* and the grey-leaved cultivars *B. macrophylla* 'Jack Frost' and 'Sea Heart' which are almost identical, but I have been told that 'Sea Heart' is stronger and grows better.

Wallflowers also think it is time to show some colour in various shades of yellow, orange, and terracotta. I have a number of species including *Erysimum* 'Red Jep' and 'Covent Garden', which grow very well and produce countless seedlings in the hottest and lightest spots in the garden.

12 Months in My Garden

JANUARY

FEBRUARY

MAY

JUNE

SEPTEMBER

OCTOBER

MARCH

APRIL

JULY

AUGUST

NOVEMBER

DECEMBER

Island beds

Lawns are normally neatly trimmed, evergreen areas hosting an occasional shrub or tree. In general, they are quite dull but that can change if, in the early months of the year, various areas in the lawn are transformed into colourful carpets. And that can easily be done with the help of spring-flowering bulbs. A solution that unites a neatly trimmed lawn with a carpet of bulbous flowers is a lawn with one or more so-called island beds. These are areas in which bulbs are planted and where they get the chance to flower, self-seed, and wither in their own rhythm, undisturbed by a lawn mower. So these bulbs will stay in the soil for years to come—you only have to plant them once.

The easiest way to create such an island bed is to plant a mixture of easy-growing bulbs like snowdrops, crocuses, and glory of the snow. But if you really aim for a spectacular effect, you should choose at least ten species which flower in consecutive weeks. In that way, your colourful carpet is changing all the time, and each phase will provide lots of pleasure.

Recipe for a ten-species colourful carpet:

Galanthus elwesii (snowdrop)
Crocus tommasinianus 'Barr's Purple' (crocus)
Crocus tommasinianus 'Ruby Giant' (crocus)
Scilla mischtschenkoana (white squill)
Chionodoxa forbesii (glory of the snow)
Muscari latifolium (grape hyacinth)
Muscari armeniacum 'Valerie Finnis' (grape hyacinth)
Narcissus 'Tête-à-Tête' (daffodil)
Narcissus 'W.P. Milner' (daffodil)
Tulipa clusiana 'Lady Jane' (wild tulip)

Order equal quantities of each species/variety and start with small numbers, for instance 50 bulbs of each. That gives you 500 bulbs to plant, for a start, which will be enough for one small island bed. Mow the future island bed area of your lawn very short before you start scattering the bulbs so that you can see where even the smallest bulbs land. Then throw all the various bulbs into a wheelbarrow, mix well, and scatter them in smaller and larger groups in the area of your lawn that you have chosen as the location for your island bed. Plant the bulbs where they fall. As mentioned before, all of them will come back in the following years. Some of them, like crocuses, glory of the snow, and grape hyacinths, will self-seed immediately, while others will take more time to naturalise.

Planting bulbs in turf is more difficult than in a border because you have to stab through the turf to make a good hole. A hole should be three times as deep as the height of the bulb. Helpful planting tools to do this are a hori hori (a Japanese knife designed to be used in the soil), a bulb trowel, or a bulb auger. After the hole has been made and the bulb put into it, cover it with a little bit of good soil.

When all the bulbs have been planted, they need moisture to be able to develop their root system. So if it does not rain, water them yourself. Once they have roots, the bulbs are frost resistant and ready for next spring. All the bulbs in the recipe mentioned above will flower in different periods, starting with snowdrops as the earliest ones and ending with the wild tulip as the latest. After the last flower has gone, the whole area of the island bed should be left undisturbed for about 5 weeks to make sure that all the bulbs have completed the full cycle of dying down. After that period, the island bed can be mowed again.

And last but not least: all spring-flowering bulbs, whether they are in borders or in island beds, need a dry period in summer to be able to prepare for next year's flowering season. Sprinkler systems are their worst enemy because they keep the soil moist. So when you choose a location for your island bed, stay away from the sprinklers!

Rosa 'Golden Wings'

Favourite Plants: Yellow

In many gardens, yellow is absolutely not used. I don't know many garden
enthusiasts who like the colour yellow. That's surprising, because there
are so many different shades of yellow that you would expect there to be
something to suit everyone's taste. I like yellow very much because it is
such a cheerful colour which oddly enough mainly appears in spring:
yellow with creamy white, yellow with orange, but also yellow with all sorts
of shades of green produce combinations that are delightful to the eye.
In my garden, April is defined by yellow in all sorts of subtle distinctions
and combined with a lot of pale green. I would have no trouble compiling
a long list of plants with yellow flowers, but I will restrict myself again to
ten favourites:

Aquilegia chrysantha 'Yellow Queen'   Coreopsis verticillata 'Moonbeam'   Crocus chrysanthus 'Cream Beauty'

Kirengeshoma palmata   Narcissus 'Swallow'   Primula elatior

Saruma henryi   Smyrnium perfoliatum   Solidaster luteus

MAY

May is a month of great promise and tremendous anticipation, with a whole gardening season to look forward to. But it's also a month of hard work to make sure the garden is as colourful and interesting as possible, with a succession of blooms right through to autumn. In other words, it's now time to plant your summer bulbs and annual flowers. Thankfully the days are nice and long this month, with plenty of bright daylight and pleasant temperatures, so it's no hardship to take the occasional break from working inside at your desk to focus on the jobs that need doing in your garden.

There Is Work to Be Done!

High on the list of priorities is pruning hedges and shrubs. This should always be done in the growing season because that's when a plant's cuts heal most quickly. Generally speaking, the growing season is from early April until late September.

You should tackle any *Buxus* shrubs first, but it's best to wait for a couple of consecutive cloudy days to avoid the freshly cut tips of the foliage burning in the sunlight. Any privet hedges that have become a little bushy need attention too. They are at their most striking when they form a neat backdrop to the abundance of spring colour that is now starting to emerge in the flower beds. They need trimming at least four or five times in the growing season, but it's a job I'm happy to do.

Beech and hornbeam hedges grow less vigorously; it's usually sufficient to prune them just twice, or sometimes three times, a year. I always try to schedule the final trim towards the end of September because the hedges will hardly produce any new growth after that, meaning they will head into the winter looking nice and tidy. The hawthorns will also need pruning twice or three times a year. If necessary, they can wait until June, but no longer than that—otherwise the plants will become too untidy, detracting from the contrast between the neat shapes and the voluminous flamboyance elsewhere in the garden.

A month of transition

May is when the early-spring bulbs are gearing up for their grand finale, while late tulips and daffodils, *Camassia*, and a handful of other blooms such as *Scilla litardierei* are still at their best. Tulips that bloom the latest and longest include *Tulipa* 'Burgundy Lace' (red), 'Flaming Parrot' (yellow with red), and 'Maureen' (white). All three of them are reliable candidates if you're looking for a tulip that will come back for several consecutive years, and 'Maureen' will even last into June. Other late-spring bulbs are

Camassia leichtlinii 'Caerulea'

Scilla litardierei

Tulipa 'Maureen'

Allium 'Beau Regard'

Allium 'Violet Beauty'

Camassia leichtlinii 'Alba'

Allium nigrum

Allium roseum

Allium ursinum

Allium zebdanense

Nectaroscordum siculum bud

Nectaroscordum siculum in flower

The blue columbine (*Aquilegia vulgaris*)

alliums (or flowering onions); this month, the onus is very much on them to add a dash of colour. In order of appearance, we have *Allium zebdanense*, *Allium nigrum*, *Allium roseum*, *Allium christophii*, *Allium* 'Beau Regard', and *Allium* 'Violet Beauty'. Bringing up the rear is Bulgarian honey garlic (*Nectaroscordum siculum*), which is actually part of the allium family too. This variety has tiny characteristic greenish-pink flowers that create a starburst effect when in bloom, but the plant is equally striking after pollination when the stems stand erect, proudly displaying their decorative seed pods.

Meanwhile, it's as if the rest of the garden is taking a breather. There is plenty of fresh new foliage—green or otherwise—from the reawakening perennials, but real colour is limited to a handful of flowering plants such as peonies, of course, as well as poppies and columbines (*Aquilegia*). In addition, there is *Geum* in warm orange and bright red, plus—more modestly—early geranium varieties such as *Geranium sylvaticum* 'Mayflower' and 'Album'. In the case of those two varieties, I always cut them back after they have flowered to encourage them to flower again later in the season.

While we're on the subject of pruning: May is also the month of the Chelsea chop—a method which entails cutting back half of the stems a perennial has produced so far. (The name came about because the best period to do this for the first time is the last week of May: the same week as the Chelsea Flower Show.) That much pruning might seem a little drastic, but it definitely benefits the plants themselves because it makes them stronger and sturdier, meaning they are less likely to topple over later in the season. Needless to say, there are all kinds of technical solutions for supporting plants, such as sticks, metal frames, or plastic netting, but in my experience those solutions are never completely invisible, meaning they detract from the overall effect.

Arrangement of three alliums: *Allium* 'Beau Regard', *Allium* 'Violet Beauty', and *Allium atropurpureum* under *Viburnum plicatum* 'Watanabe'

The so-called Chelsea chop carried out on *Campanula lactiflora* 'Loddon Anna'

Not all types of plants can withstand the Chelsea chop, but phlox, tall campanulas such as *Campanula lactiflora* 'Loddon Anna', asters, *Coreopsis tripteris*, *Kalimeris incisa*, and *Artemisia* varieties such as *Artemisia pontica* will definitely thrive on it. You can choose whether to cut back the entire plant by half in one go or to thin out just a third or half of the stems first and then do the rest another time—in which case the plant will flower several times over a longer period (and that has its upside, of course). Personally, I cut back *Campanula lactiflora* 'Loddon Anna' a number of times, which results in the first shoots flowering in June and the final ones not until August.

Annuals and summer bulbs

In May, I always plan in a couple of days for garden-related jobs. After all, besides all the pruning that has to be done, May is also the month for putting in all the summer bulbs and annual plants. The chance of frost has passed once we get to the second half of May—despite gardeners in many European countries believing that the Ice Saints can still bring cold weather from May 11 to 15—and we no longer have to worry about a young plant's susceptibility to frost.

Pot of summer plants made up of white *Bidens ferulifolia* 'Bellamy White', silver-leaved *Helichrysum petiolare* 'Silver', and red *Salvia* 'Wendy's Wish'

Our own garden has become so full that there's hardly any room for annual summer-flowering plants, plus our slightly heavier clay soil is far from ideal for getting annuals off to a good start, which is why I mainly plant annuals in pots and tubs. The spring bulbs in the pots are nearing their end towards mid-May, so I tip those bulbs onto the compost heap. After all, leaving them in their pots until the following year rarely results in them flowering again.

The beginning of early summer in the garden with columbine, smyrnium, and the late-flowering white camassia

I'll occasionally see a few grape hyacinths or the odd daffodil, but I tend to plant new bulbs in my pots every autumn, and so I can now use all those pots and tubs to plant summer flowers.

First of all, it's important to clean the insides of the pots thoroughly. I subsequently put in new potting soil, including fertiliser, mixed with some coarse sand for drainage, and then I pot the new plants in anticipation of a long, colourful summer. That's not quite the whole story, however, because these kinds of plants—which have just one season to show us what they're capable of—need a lot of nutrients. In the first few weeks

Salvia uliginosa

Gaura lindheimeri 'Whirling Butterflies'

Dahlia 'Giraffe'

Lilium 'Scheherazade'

Lilium 'African Queen'

Lilium 'Casa Blanca'

they obtain everything they need from the potting mix, but after that they need a helping hand. In other words, as soon as they have reached the peak flowering phase, they should be fertilised once a week with a special summer-flowering mix to ensure that they stay in optimal condition right through to the end of the summer.

For now, when the plants are still small and surrounded by a relatively large area of bare earth, I cover the surface with grass cuttings—a method also known as mulching. You can do the same with a freshly planted border if a lot of space is still visible in between the plants. The grass helps to keep the soil moist and prevents weeds from taking hold.

The only annuals that develop well when planted in our garden—and sometimes even come back the following year after a mild winter—are

Salvia uliginosa, with its sky-blue flowers loved by bees, *Gaura lind-heimeri*, which is a mass of delicate white butterfly-like flowers right through to November, and *Verbena rigida* 'Venosa', with its haze of purple flowers. With a bit of luck they reappear every spring, so they are more like perennials really.

In addition to the annual summer-flowering plants, there's a big group of summer bulbs that are native to subtropical or tropical climates. While they generally thrive in our summers, they can't cope with freezing temperatures, which means that you have to replant them every year. The best-known summer bulbs are dahlias, begonias, and lilies. Personally, I'm a big fan of dahlias because they last for months, and there are so many different varieties that you can always find one with the right colour and effect for every type of border. Much to my dismay, however, dahlias just can't survive in my garden; slugs and snails devour them every time. After several failed attempts and the use of slug pellets and coffee grounds to no avail, I've given up. Lilies are no good either because they get ravaged by lily beetles. I've heard that it helps if you plant the lilies in a windy spot, but our garden is very sheltered so that's not an option in our case. The only two varieties that do have some degree of success, although in the second year much less so than the first, are *Lilium* × *testaceum* and *Lilium martagon*. It's small consolation, but I'm grateful to have anything at all. So I use my favourite summer bulbs wherever they can play a leading role in other projects.

My favourites are:

Cosmos atrosanguineus   *Dahlia* 'Honka White'
Gladiolus murielae   *Dahlia* 'Karma Lagoon'
Lilium 'African Queen'   *Dahlia* 'Happy Single Wink'
Lilium 'Casa Blanca'   *Ornithogalum saundersiae*
Lilium 'Scheherazade'   *Triteleia* 'Rudy'
Dahlia 'Giraffe'

Gladiolus murielae

Crocosmia (*Montbretia*) is officially a summer bulb too, even though this variety can withstand frost. Once it has been planted and starts to grow, *Crocosmia* acts like a perennial. It actually thrives far too well in our soil, resulting in explosive growth. Many years ago I planted several varieties of bulbs including *Crocosmia* 'Lucifer' and 'Fire King' and *Crocosmia* × *crocosmiiflora* 'George Davison', but I've ripped many of them out again since because they started to encroach on all the surrounding plants and rapidly produced thick clusters of new bulbs. I now keep a close eye on them and intervene as soon as necessary, because I don't really want to get rid of them altogether. With their ornate foliage and long-lasting flowers, sometimes followed by decorative seeds, I regard them as an essential part of my summer borders.

Another summer-flowering bulb that has been coming back for the past few years, much to my surprise, is *Cosmos atrosanguineus*, the chocolate cosmos. It's a bit of a slow starter, but it's beautiful when it finally blooms. The only summer bulb that I plant every year, both in the soil and in tubs and pots, is *Gladiolus murielae*, the Abyssinian gladiolus, because of its exquisite flowers and leaves as well as its heady fragrance. I plant the bulbs at several intervals from mid-May to mid-June so that the flowering period lasts as long as possible at the end of the summer and into early autumn.

I've had a lot more success with summer annuals and summer bulbs when working on various projects throughout the Netherlands. In 2012, I had the privilege of planting part of the Borders of the 20th and 21st Century project with seasonal plants at Akerendam House in Beverwijk. Beyond my section, which was in the middle of a lawn, you could see borders by Piet Oudolf on either side, so I chose colours that teamed well with them. Purples, pinks, dark reds, and a splash of white ensured an exuberant display all summer long!

Summer borders at Huis Akerendam in Beverwijk

Spring and summer border at the Open Air Museum in Arnhem

Another project I did was at the Holland Open Air Museum in Arnhem, where I was tasked with designing a large, crescent-shaped seasonal border just inside the entrance, next to the Amsterdam area. The border was in front of a large, sandy-coloured storage shed with big, dark brown doors. I decided to use that as the basis for my colour scheme for the summer border, so I chose lots of reds and rich oranges with splashes of dark brown and sky-blue on a green base. The end result is another reminder of the importance of factoring in the surroundings when choosing the colours of your plants and flowers. Rather than being individual elements, the backdrop and the plants work together as one to create a unified effect.

Full bloom ahead in May

Besides the hawthorns, other trees that blossom in May include the *Prunus serrula* with its splendid bark and the multi-stemmed *Magnolia obovata*. The *Prunus* blossoms quite subtly, so you might not even notice that it's in flower until it's too late, when the petals form a carpet of white blossom on the surface of our pond. You have to look carefully to spot magnolia blossoms too, because the buds are partially hidden by the big, oval leaves. They gradually become more visible as the flowers open and gain more volume. People often don't realise that our magnolia is a magnolia because its foliage is very different, with leaves up to 45 cm long and 15 cm wide. As an added bonus, the leaves can be dried and then—just like grape leaves, for example—used to wrap up food for the barbecue, such as fish, meat, or certain kinds of vegetables. The delicious aromatic leaves subtly infuse the filling with extra flavour.

Tulipa 'Peppermint Stick'

12 Months in My Garden

JANUARY

FEBRUARY

MAY

JUNE

SEPTEMBER

OCTOBER

MARCH

APRIL

JULY

AUGUST

NOVEMBER

DECEMBER

Zinnia marylandica 'Double Zahara Fire'

Favourite Plants: Orange

Orange is one of those colours that people often steer clear of. It's true that bright orange, such as the colour of marigolds, can be garish and overbearing, but softer shades of orange can look distinguished and work really well in combination with yellows, russets, and bright greens. Orange is a common colour in bulbs, roses, and summer-flowering annuals, whereas there are only a few orange varieties of perennials. I've listed ten of my orange favourites from all of these categories below:

Alstroemeria 'Indian Summer'

Cosmos sulphureus

Crocosmia × crocosmiiflora 'George Davison'

Euphorbia griffithii 'Fireglow'

Fritillaria imperialis 'Bach'

Lilium lancifolium

Lilium 'Orange Cocotte'

Papaver cambricum

Rosa 'Westerland'

JUNE

My first visit to gardens in England was in 1977: I went for about
5 days, and we visited at least four gardens every day. When I
returned, my head was full to bursting with all the combinations
and individual new species I had learned about in England. They
included wallflowers, which I had been practically unfamiliar with
until then. They were everywhere, even in the smallest front gardens, in all sorts of different colours and with enviable names,
such as *Erysimum* 'Primrose Dame' (pale yellow with creamy
white), *Erysimum* 'Apricot Twist' (also known as 'Apricot Delight';
apricot-orange), and *Erysimum cheiri* 'Fire King' (orange-red).
My love for wallflowers continues to this day, for various reasons:
their tendency to flower on and on, their heavenly scent, their
evergreen appearance, and their ability to thrive in the driest,
sunniest spots.

The Early Bird Catches the Worm

By June, wallflowers are past their peak in terms of flowering, but they carry on producing flowers—sometimes more, sometimes fewer—all summer long. I can monitor them closely because, of course, our borders had to have wallflowers too, even though the soil is actually too rich for them. I have planted them on the edges of the gravel path as much as possible, where the soil is a bit drier and poorer quality. They reseed there in abundance. In other places, towards the middle of the border, they really become too spindly, but as long as they don't give up completely, I just leave them there. The best place for wallflowers is at the edge of a hot, dry, sunny border, such as at the entrance to our garden, under the letterboxes. I planted seedlings from the garden there and they took straight away; now they are wedged between a concrete path and a wooden shed. They have become strong, compact bushes in this apparently ideal spot, revealing their first terracotta flowers in February and continuing to flower far into the summer.

Tinkering with flowering

Work in the garden continues unabated throughout June. I really have to plan my days to avoid the work becoming overwhelming: the momentum which gathered at the beginning of May as perennials developed now seems to be a seething mass which will only calm down at the end of this month. That means going through the garden every day, checking to see that nothing has gone astray and whether timely action is needed. *Smyrnium perfoliatum* has now finished flowering and has produced little black seeds which can be collected and given to other people who are fond of this plant. The remaining golden yellow stems can be pulled out easily at the same time as the last yellowing leaves of the spring-flowering bulbs.

Erysimum 'Red Jep'   *Erysimum* 'Bowles' Mauve'

That reveals the first stubborn weeds, including shrubby bindweed and ground elder, and you need to spend some time tackling it.

Just like May, June is a month in which you will often reach for your hedge-clippers and secateurs. The first are to neaten up your hedges, because they form the framework for the luxuriant plants in the borders. The tidier it all looks, the better. Now that the borders have become so full, I'm pleased I decided to leave an open space (about 40–50 cm wide) between the hedge and the border when I laid out the garden: it is a strip of soil with no plants in it so I can always get close to the hedge to trim it and the clippings fall onto this pathway. It is very frustrating when hedge clippings fall straight into a border, and you have to put a lot of effort into clearing them up without damaging the border plants. The secateurs are needed when early-flowering geraniums, such as *Geranium* × *magnificum* and *Geranium macrorrhizum*, finish flowering. If you cut them right down to the ground, they will produce new leaves within a few days which look attractive all summer.

I do the same to the aquilegia and lady's mantle: cut them right back and new leaves will soon appear. I cut other flowering plants back again and again later in the season to encourage new growth. I mentioned *Campanula lactiflora* 'Loddon Anna' before, but *Veronica longifolia* 'Marietta' and *Veronicastrum virginicum* 'Album' also form new buds when the old flowers are cut off.

Certain shrubs don't escape a pruning round this month either. Quite a number of shrubs that flower in spring have to be cut back immediately after they have flowered because they develop flowers on last year's wood. I cut off the branches of the lilacs, *Deutzia*, and mock orange in my garden after they have flowered to stimulate new growth and flowers next year.

To continue on the theme of pruning for a moment: the hawthorns which grow between the public garden and our private gardens are also due a trim in June. Trimming these shrubs is a job that requires some skill. You have to manoeuvre from the top of a ladder placed carefully in the borders below. I steer clear of using electric hedge-clippers at such a height anymore, but luckily our neighbours' youngest son, Toon, is very handy with them. I'm happy to leave it up to him.

He is also the person who helps me to prune the evergreen Delavay privet (*Ligustrum delavayanum*) which towers above one of the sunniest borders like a parasol. Pruning this shrub into shape is quite a skill: Toon balances on a stepladder as he prunes, and I stand as close as possible with an umbrella held upside-down to stop the cuttings from ending up in the border or the gravel. This method ensures that the cuttings fall into the umbrella, enabling me to empty it easily into a big wheelbarrow.

Pruning the parasol-shaped Delavay privet with the help of my neighbour's son, Toon, and an upside-down umbrella

Veronicastrum virginicum 'Album'

Campanula lactiflora 'Loddon Anna'

Smyrnium perfoliatum with *Helleborus orientalis*

Modifying and smartening up

I don't just monitor plant development in my own garden, but also in other projects where I was responsible for the planting plan. In 2008–2009 I worked on planting plans for the National Perennial Plants Theme Garden in the Gardens of Appeltern, which opened in 2010. Since then, I go there at least once a year to do the rounds and check on it, accompanied by the supplier of the perennials and the gardener responsible for looking after the garden. You learn a lot from doing the rounds, because you see how the plants are developing and where modifications are required. Now, years later, some borders are in need of renovation. Because all three of us have monitored them in recent years, it's fairly easy to come to an agreement on any modifications.

It's a different story when it comes to the project for the Amerongen Castle flower garden. When I visited the garden on a trip organised by the magazine *Onze Eigen Tuin*, I was approached by a volunteer who worked in the Amerongen Castle gardens. She told me that the castle had received a sum of money left in a will which expressed the desire for it to be used to turn the neglected cut-flower garden into a contemporary flower garden. She asked me if I would be interested in taking a look sometime. So, one sunny Monday afternoon in September, I met the head gardener and the volunteers responsible for this new development. We discussed the options, looked at the site, and I eventually went home with a new assignment.

It took a winter to finalise the plans and dig up the old garden, modify it, and finally make it ready for planting. But by the end of March the following year, we were ready and able to set to work. I started by setting out the plants; fairly quickly after that, everyone understood what to do and the whole garden was planted in no time. Two months later, I was back to oversee the planting of the dahlias. The flower garden was then ready for its first colourful season. Because new soil mixed with compost had been added to the borders, some plants, such as *Agastache*, reacted

Veronica longifolia 'Marietta' with *Lavatera olbia* 'Rosea'

Cluster of *Deutzia* flowers

Magenta *Geranium psilostemon* with *Allium* 'Beau Regard' and pale blue *Geranium pratense* 'Mrs Kendall Clark'

Campanula lactiflora 'Loddon Anna'

The beginning and end of May in the Gardens of Appeltern

July and August in the Gardens of Appeltern

Summer in the flower garden at Amerongen Castle

by producing enormous bushes. But it was certainly colourful and, over time, the plants would restore their balance. The last activity in that same year was to plant mixtures of spring-flowering bulbs; I worked with the same group of volunteers again who seemed to become more enthusiastic every time.

Nowadays, I go there a couple of times a year to see what is happening, give advice, and answer questions. I like being able to keep a finger on the pulse in this way, and the volunteers know that there is always someone in the background they can consult. That guarantees the highest possible quality.

Agastache 'Blue Fortune'

Early mornings

One of the most delightful aspects of the month of June is that it starts getting light just after four o'clock in the morning. As soon as the birds start singing and it looks as though it's going to be a nice day, I just have to get out of bed and take a look at the garden. The garden is at its best in the soft morning light, and the intense scent some plants emit (such as *Campanula lactiflora* 'Loddon Anna' yet again) is at its purest. Those few hours before the rest of the world comes to life give me enough energy and inspiration for another busy day, and that's why I really love June.

Surprises

One of this month's surprises is the appearance of the late-flowering bulbs I'd forgotten I had planted. One of them was *Ixia paniculata* 'Eos' which appeared at the edge of the round border in between the *Geranium macrorrhizum*. I had visualised something quite different: the flowers that emerged were a bit spotty and untidy instead of the creamy yellow stars I had envisaged. Perhaps the position had something to do with it or there was too much competition from surrounding plants which prevented them from developing to the full? I'd just have to wait and see if they would do better next year and, if not, too bad.

Geranium macrorrhizum 'Spessart'

Towards the middle of the same border, leaves and buds of *Ornithogalum ponticum* 'Sochi' emerged in mid-June. The buds developed into long, pyramid-shaped clusters of pure white flowers, 60 cm tall, and each bulb even produced several flowers. It was a fantastic acquisition which continued to flower for 6 weeks.

I stumbled across the delicate white and sky-blue flowers of *Triteleia* more or less by accident as they bravely pushed their way through the surrounding perennials in the border next to the greenhouse. They flowered sparingly in the first year, but they are in an ideal spot in so many ways: in the sun, in the driest border in the garden, and with a warm wall behind them. That bodes well for the coming years.

To stay with bulbs: June is also the month to replant bulbs which hardly produced any flowers in the spring. That often happens with daffodils and *Camassia* when they form bulb offsets which are too big for the individual bulbs to develop well any longer. Bulb offsets are baby bulbs of the original bulb which have developed into new bulbs. If that happens year after year, you get larger clumps of bulbs growing on each other; they

There's so much to see in summer. Everything is doing its utmost to look its best.

have to be divided every few years so that they can flower continuously. Sometimes a lack of light can cause fewer flowers: bulbs that were planted near a small bush 5 years ago can end up in the shade of a bush that has grown large and that has repercussions for the lushness of their flowers.

June is the perfect time to dig these bulbs up because you can see where they are by their yellowing leaves. So dig them up carefully, separate the bulb offsets, and then replant the individual bulbs separately in large and small groups in places where they will get more light. The second bulb task this month is to order new bulbs for the following autumn. If you

Ixia paniculata 'Eos'

Triteleia laxa 'Koningin Fabiola'

order bulbs early you won't run the risk later in the season of finding that all sorts of species are no longer available. Set aside some time to consult your notes from last spring, make a list, and place the order. Then at least you can be sure that you'll get what you want in autumn.

Sleeping beauty

Many years ago, a friend and I went to the Journées des Plantes in Courson, a famous plant fair just south of Paris (although it has now been moved to Domaine de Chantilly, north of Paris). At the end of the day, we were strolling past all the beautiful plants and, after thinking long and hard, my friend decided to buy the climbing rose she had been admiring earlier in the day. And so we returned home with a rose labelled 'King Edward VII' in the boot of the car.

She planted it against a sunny façade on Transvaalkade in Amsterdam, surrounded by grey paving stones, but that didn't discourage it. It resolutely began its climb up the façade, grasping onto wire cables which had to be moved higher up again and again. After about 4 years, when the rose had almost reached the top floor, it was too much for my friend and she decided that the rose had to go. That was a pity, because when it flowered, the whole house looked like Sleeping Beauty's castle: covered in huge

A magnificent summer arrangement of *Allium* 'Violet Beauty', *Ornithogalum ponticum* 'Sochi', and *Euphorbia seguieriana* subsp. *niciciana*, whose flower heads have gone to seed

clusters of white roses—very romantic. But I promised I would take it over; I had plenty of room and that helped to soften the blow.

I still don't know how she managed to get it out of the ground, but the rose arrived in my garden with enough roots and few good main branches. I planted it next to the ash, but that didn't suit it, so I moved it to the dike to entwine around the handrail of the stairs to the top of the dike. That wasn't a success either, because the new shoots were so long that you soon couldn't go up or down the steps unscathed. So I had to replant the rose again, and it tore in two. I planted it on top of the dike, next to the brambles where it was finally happy. The bramble bushes gave it something to get hold of, and they gradually disappeared under a blanket of roses. It is

The climbing rose, labelled as 'King Edward VII', that wouldn't stop growing in its original home in Amsterdam and in my garden in Weesp

now so big that the rose's tentacles are reaching across the brambles and hanging over the hawthorn on the dike like lianas. It looks wonderful and impressive, but when will it stop?

And the strange thing about this story is that I am not really a fan of roses at all. I usually find them to be too formal and stiff, and they don't go with the predominantly graceful plants that have become my trademark. There are only a few I can really appreciate, including *Rosa rugosa* 'Fru Dagmar Hastrup' because of its wonderful scent, *Rosa* 'Westerland' because of its copper colour, and *Rosa chinensis* 'Mutabilis' because it displays a multitude of colours from pale yellow to deep strawberry-pink as it develops from bud to full flower.

Rosa 'Westerland'
in full bloom

12 Months in My Garden

JANUARY

FEBRUARY

MAY

JUNE

SEPTEMBER

OCTOBER

MARCH

APRIL

JULY

AUGUST

NOVEMBER

DECEMBER

Alcea rosea

Favourite Plants: Red

There are many shades of red, but my favourite is the true bright red, sometimes also called tomato red or fire engine red. That colour of red attracts attention, so you need to use it sparingly, because it makes all the other colours pale into insignificance. Bright red looks its best amongst bright green, so many ornamental grasses are eligible as companions. But true red also looks attractive against the lilac-grey shades of lavender, for instance, or *Verbena rigida* 'Polaris'. And this bright colour unashamedly peps up a pink border which has a tendency to look greyish in bright sunlight. Sparks will fly with the following species:

Bidens ferulifolia Hawaiian Flare 'Red Drop'

Crocosmia 'Lucifer'

Dahlia 'Honka Surprise'

Lobelia speciosa 'Fan Red'

Paeonia 'Red Charm'

Potentilla 'Arc-en-ciel'

Ricinus communis 'Carmencita Red'

Tagetes patula 'Burning Embers'

Tulipa 'Leo'

BORDER OF ANNUALS

If you have an empty space in your garden or if you have
a brand-new garden, a border of annuals can be a fast fix
to cheer it up with plenty of colour. It is best to give a border like this some structure as well as colour by adding
annual ornamental grasses, for instance, or other species
of foliage plants.

Taste is a personal matter of course, but I have chosen
orange and yellow—which are often sneered at—for one
border and softened their flamboyance with foliage plants
(ornamental grasses and sage). The border drawn here has
an area of about 9 m². If you assume about 15 plants/m²,
you will need a total of 135 plants. Put the foliage plants
in first, mixed up, spread over the entire area, and leave
different-sized spaces in between. Fill in the spaces with
a random mixture of the flowering plants.

✳ = 17 PENNISETUM GLAUCUM 'JADE PRINCESS'
o = 45 RUDBECKIA HIRTA 'GOLDILOCKS'
◯ = 8 BIDENS FERULIFOLIA 'HAWAIIAN FLAIR'

OP ALLE OVERGEBLEVEN PLEKKEN EEN WILLEKEURIG
GEMENGDE MIX VAN:

15 PANICUM VIRGATUM 'FONTAINE'
20 SALVIA OFFICINALIS 'ICTERINA'
25 TAGETES PATULA 'DISCO RED'

Pennisetum glaucum 'Jade Princess'

Bidens ferulifolia 'Hawaiian Flare'

Rudbeckia hirta 'Goldilocks'

Panicum virgatum 'Fontaine'

Salvia officinalis 'Icterina'

Tagetes patula 'Disco Red'

JULY

When my garden was only a couple of years old and the borders
hadn't filled up completely, regular visitors occasionally gave
me presents of plants from their own gardens. They did so with
the best intentions, but it didn't always turn out well. I still blame
myself for not looking more closely at that one clump of pink
phlox I was given. After a year, it turned out that the clump contained a stowaway. I only discovered it once the little plant—the
dreaded ground elder—had started to roam around the border
where I'd planted the phlox. I still fight this intruder as soon as
I see it pop up. By removing the leaves as often as possible, the
plants eventually become worn out. I'm hoping I am now finally
going to see the results of my efforts. After all, slow and steady
wins the race, but I'd rather put my energy into something else.

Peace and Quiet

As June turns into July, the garden finally quietens down. The exuberance of spring has made way for more modest green, out of which surprises emerge from time to time. The sunniest borders look very bright with the almost luminous green of the spurges, including *Euphorbia seguieriana* subsp. *niciciana* and *Euphorbia schillingii*. They form a good background colour for the amber and red of *Crocosmia* × *crocosmiiflora* 'George Davison' and *Crocosmia* 'Lucifer', but also for the wispy *Gaura lindheimeri* which flowers for months and likes to mix in this company.

Phloxes, hydrangeas, and various *Geranium* species alternate in the shadier borders, interrupted here and there by a sturdy clump of *Calamagrostis*, which bends with every breath of wind, or a tuft of St John's wort (*Hypericum* × *inodorum* 'Elstead'). Both species hold their characteristic shape until well into winter; that makes them indispensable as a basis for a border which has to remain attractive for as long as possible.

Even the very darkest border is looking its best. The lace cap hydrangeas (*Hydrangea macrophylla* 'Mariesii') are now at their prettiest, and the slugs haven't yet discovered the imposing hostas. In between, an interesting interaction can be seen of leaf and flower shapes belonging, amongst others, to *Rodgersia*, the first Japanese anemones, and a fountain of *Epilobium angustifolium* 'Album' (white rosebay willowherb) in the background. The last one is a species you have to keep an eye on, because if you're not careful, it will take over the whole border. To prevent that from happening, I remove a large number of shoots every year. Then I enjoy seeing it reappear year after year in the very same place, where it towers above the surrounding perennials and becomes the centre of attention for a couple of weeks.

All in all, July is a month in which the garden recovers its balance and in which, apart from the odd explosion of colour, leaf shapes and structures become important again. A month, too, in which looking after

Euphorbia schillingii

Crocosmia × crocosmiiflora 'George Davison'

Crocosmia 'Lucifer'

Gaura lindheimeri 'Whirling Butterflies'

Phlox paniculata 'Blue Paradise'

Epilobium angustifolium

Astilbe 'Deutschland'

Hydrangea sargentiana

Hakonechloa macra

Hypericum × inodorum 'Elstead'

Hydrangea macrophylla 'Mariesii'

Pond with *Cleome* 'Señorita Blanca' in the foreground

Acanthus spinosus   *Euphorbia seguieriana* subsp. *niciciana* in the foreground

the borders can be largely forgotten, because all the plants have grown towards each other so much that there is hardly any room for weeds, and the thick canopy of leaves keeps the soil sufficiently damp. That is unless climate change upsets everything, bringing longer and longer periods of drought and heat, alternating occasionally with heavy, monsoon-like rain showers. We will have to wait and see how our species—which are used to more traditional Dutch weather—will react.

Watering

It's the 'in' thing at the moment: owners of almost all the new gardens I become involved in want a built-in irrigation system. 'So easy. Now there's no need to lug watering cans or hosepipes around.' There's a grain of truth in this, of course, but I always find it extraordinary that many people think you can only keep a garden in prime condition with the aid of a computer. The downside of the convenience is that a computer-driven irrigation system almost always gives the garden too much water because it starts working at times when it isn't really necessary.

My strategy is only to water in emergencies: when the garden is so dry that the plants themselves start letting you know that they need water by hanging limply. That is the moment to turn on the garden spray—but do it once only, for an extended period of a couple of hours. We have installed a number of water tapping points in our garden and attached them to a pump which draws water from the nearby ditch. A hosepipe with a spray head can be connected to these tapping points and, of course, we do have to lug the hosepipe around, but we only have to do that two or three times, at most, every summer.

There are various opinions on when it is the right moment to give water: I belong to the group that thinks that early morning is the best time, while the plants are still fresh after the previous, possibly cool, night. But there is another group of garden enthusiasts who swears by watering in the evening, because the water won't then evaporate after spraying. My only advice is to try both methods for yourself and see which one works best.

Another argument against installing a computer-driven irrigation system is its bad influence on bulbs you want to naturalise. Such bulbs, which logically remain in the ground, need a dry period in order to be able to flower again the next year. If they are regularly drenched with water, which keeps the soil damper than they are used to, they will give up. That is disastrous for all your lawns and borders with snowdrops, crocuses, daffodils, and other bulbs you want to naturalise and a good reason to think carefully about whether you really want an irrigation system.

Kirengeshoma palmata

Luminous plants

July, when the borders are full, is the best time to see the difference between the light and dark spots in the garden. You can also see how using luminous plants–plants with light-coloured flowers or variegated foliage–can give these dark places more depth and improve them three-dimensionally. Variegated foliage here means that the leaves have a different colour than ordinary green: often they are chartreuse-yellow or green with a white or yellow edge or markings.

Our border against the dike is the very darkest in the garden because it is in the shade of hawthorn bushes, tall brambles, and a huge beech tree. I have put in plants there such as *Aruncus dioicus*, which produces

Plants with a variegated leaf provide light in dark spots, such as *Hosta sieboldiana* 'Frances Williams' on the left and *Brunnera macrophylla* 'Sea Heart' on the right.

creamy-white flowers in June and July, followed by the pure white flowers of *Thalictrum delavayi* 'Splendide White' and *Persicaria filiformis* 'Alba'. Variegated leaves are represented by *Brunnera macrophylla* 'Sea Heart' (greyish), *Hydrangea macrophylla* 'Variegata' (white-edged leaf and white flowers), and *Hakonechloa macra* 'Albostriata', an ornamental grass with a thin white stripe down the centre of the leaf. If you repeat these luminous species in various places in the border, it will gain perspective: your eye is drawn to the lighter spots, and you therefore perceive more depth than if the plants were plain green. And it makes the border look much more interesting.

Ice flowers

Because July is the month in which there isn't much to do in the garden, at long last there is time to do other things connected with plants or flowers. It's my birthday in July, and my birthday parties have contained a surprise element on several occasions now in the form of 'drinks in ice flowers'. I stole the idea from Martha Stewart, who put forward ideas for festive lunches and dinners for small and large groups of guests in her book, *Entertaining*, written in 1982. Flowers play an important part in these festivities, and they are incorporated in the most fantastic ways.

I was inspired by a photo of two bottles of vodka encased in blocks of ice studded with roses and sprigs of box. It all looks very festive and is really easy to make. First, place two bottles of spirits in two empty 1.5-L milk cartons, and fill the cartons with water. Drop flowers into the water and then freeze the whole lot for at least 24 hours. When you're ready to serve the spirits, peel off the cartons and place the two blocks of flower-studded ice on large trays to catch the water as it melts.

Spirits in ice flowers, copied from Martha Stewart

Summer flowers in the Royal Mile

Every year, in the middle of summer, I recall one of the best projects I ever worked on: the Royal Mile in Apeldoorn in 2008. As part of the celebrations for Triennial Apeldoorn, a showcase for gardens, culture, and landscapes, I was asked to be the main designer and supervisor of the Royal Mile, a mile-long (1.6-km) flower border. The proposed location was a dream: a paved footpath from the entrance to Park Berg en Bos that merged into a sandy path into the woods. The idea was to plant borders with perennials in the first section, on either side of the paved path. They ended at a small square where the sandy path started and the long line continued. Borders had to be created on both sides of this sandy path too, filled with summer flowers and summer-flowering bulbs, such as dahlias and lilies. The borders with perennials were laid in June 2007 and, thanks to a hot but humid summer, the plants shot up. As a result, these borders looked gorgeous and reasonably mature in 2008.

We used a different process for the border of annuals along the sandy path. I designed ten beds, five on either side of the path, in colours which

Details of two of the ten borders on the Royal Mile in Park Berg en Bos in Apeldoorn. On the left, Jane Schul's bright orange border with the emphasis on dahlias and, on the right, my own silver and lilac border featuring foliage plants.

would blend into one another. The sunniest side of the path was to have the bright colours: purple, red, bright orange, bright green, and white. Opposite them, the shadier border would be filled with softer colours: lilac, pink, pale orange, pale yellow, and grey with green. Nine other planting experts and designers, from the Netherlands and abroad, were asked to choose plants for these beds so that, in addition to my own arrangement for one of the beds, nine other plans were put into practice.

The whole process was tremendous fun. It started in June 2007, when we all went to look at the location and then discussed the conditions attached. After that, everyone set to work, because the plans had to be submitted in September to give the suppliers time to gather all the species together and/or to seed in time. Two suppliers had been selected, one for the summer-flowering bulbs and one for the annuals. The plan worked like a dream, because both parties contributed their expertise in different areas, for example giving preference to dahlias and advice on the best possible composition of the soil.

The edges of the woods were cut back in the winter of 2007/2008—as they would have been as part of the regular maintenance—and then five beds with slightly raised wooden rims were constructed along either side of the sandy path, each measuring 70 × 5 m. By mid-May 2008 everything was ready for planting, and we spent 5 days filling two beds a day. The designer whose bed was to be planted laid out the plants and a team of planters took responsibility for actually planting them. After 4 days of magnificent early-summer weather and a final day of pouring rain, everything was planted and the spectacle could begin. And it was a spectacle, fortunately, thanks to the rain in July, heat in August, and not forgetting regular, professional management.

The Royal Mile was a great success, particularly because of this section, the temporary borders—temporary because we had agreed that the old situation with the path through the woods would be restored again after one season. People still talk to me about this project, and if I am ever asked whether there is a dream assignment I wish for, I immediately think of this Royal Mile.

View of the Royal Mile showing the merging of colours in the borders

12 Months in My Garden

JANUARY

FEBRUARY

MAY

JUNE

SEPTEMBER

OCTOBER

MARCH

APRIL

JULY

AUGUST

NOVEMBER

DECEMBER

Cosmos bipinnatus

Favourite Plants: Summer-flowering Annuals

This is the month when all the plants that don't survive a Dutch winter and which we therefore call annuals finally get the chance to appear in the spotlight. The range of such plants has grown tremendously in the last 20 years. That means we are no longer limited to the traditional bedding plants such as wax begonias, marigolds, and red salvia, but can make full use of a large group of more modern plants which look lighter, more frivolous, and sometimes unusual and which invite us to experiment in all sorts of ways. My favourites in this group are:

Amaranthus cruentus 'Hot Biscuits'

Begonia Crackling Fire® Creamy Yellow

Bidens ferulifolia 'Bellamy White'

Caladium 'White Queen'

Cleome 'Sparkler'

Erigeron karvinskianus

Gladiolus murielae

Nicotiana sylvestris

Pennisetum setaceum 'Rubrum'

AUGUST

Gardens didn't really interest me when I was a child. My memories of August are mainly filled with the enormous quantities of French beans, broad beans, and lettuces my father brought in from his vegetable garden. I have a vague memory of the border next to our house and my mother occasionally tackling the weeds there. But I only started enjoying a garden properly much later when I first got a garden of my own. I became enthralled by it and never had enough space because I wanted to plant far too many unusual plants.

Huge Enjoyment

Lack of space is still an issue because the garden in Weesp has gradually filled up too. It's really difficult to find room for new acquisitions. A first-world problem! But apart from that, August is the month to enjoy to the full, because after all the activity in previous months, the plants have gradually stabilised. The time has come when obligations can take a back seat and you can look with satisfaction at the continual surprising developments and combinations.

The hydrangeas have just passed their peak flowering period. Their flowers are fading and gradually changing into paper-like structures which will be worth looking at well into the winter. The same applies to numerous other plants which are still looking their best at the moment: *Verbena bonariensis*, for instance, and *Sedum* 'Matrona', *Veronicastrum*, and *Hypericum × inodorum* 'Elstead', which flaunts its branches of first red and then black berries right until you prune it in February.

This is the month in which I have relatively little work to do in the garden. The most important tasks involve regularly watering the pots of summer-flowering plants and giving them extra feed. And if the

Verbena bonariensis with *Persicaria amplexicaulis*

Sedum 'Matrona' with *Artemisia* 'Powis Castle' and *Imperata cylindrica* 'Red Baron'

temperatures go sky-high, it's a good idea to keep an eye on any plants which might need an additional drink. I turn on the garden spray as little as possible, on the assumption that the plants ought to be able to look after themselves. But if they really hang limply for a prolonged period, it's time to act. August is mainly the month to dream about what else is possible: the garden always seems to give me input in one way or another, including for other projects.

Midsummer is also the time in which I enjoy visiting other gardens and nurseries—preferably several times—to be inspired, such as the Open Days at Volmary, a nursery for summer annuals, just over the border in Münster, Germany. The experimental fields are in flower in August, and you need a long day to see everything. The *Sichtungsgarten* (viewing garden) in Weihenstephan, southern Germany, is another; you learn a lot there because they conduct all sorts of experiments with assortments. And while you are traveling around Germany, there is bound to be a *Bundesgartenschau* or *Landesgartenschau* (horticultural show) to visit where there is plenty to see and learn. The Germans are especially good at plant arrangements of summer annuals for public green spaces. Their approach is rather more conventional than ours in the Netherlands, but always useful for new inspiration.

I twice had the opportunity of designing part of a *Landesgartenschau*: in Bad Essen in 2010 and in Papenburg in 2014. In Bad Essen, I designed the borders around Schloss Ippenburg. In Papenburg, I was assigned one of the twelve themed gardens with the theme of ebb and flow, chosen because of the many shipyards in Papenburg. Both were interesting projects, and I acquired a wealth of experience. The day before I was due to plant my summer plants in Papenburg, I discovered that the order for my garden hadn't been sent to the suppliers. Huge panic—what now? With an enormous amount of help from the person in charge of the gardens, we were able to find the large majority of the summer flowers in the colours I wanted (blue and white) at a variety of regional nurseries and garden centres. But unfortunately, they were all bedding plants, no taller than

View of the Volmary nursery

Schloss Ippenburg in Bad Essen

Landesgartenschau (garden festival) in Papenburg

Salvia uliginosa

Salvia guaranitica 'Black and Blue' with the plumes of
Pennisetum orientale 'Karley Rose'

Summer annuals and summer-flowering bulbs

The 'green lung' in the centre of Arnhem

30 cm. Because I also needed higher features, I phoned my friend Fleur van Zonneveld who owns the nursery De Kleine Plantage an hour's drive away from Papenburg. She was able to help me out with the jewels for my planting plan: *Salvia uliginosa*, *Salvia guaranitica*, and *Verbena bonariensis*. And so everything worked out well in the end.

The French are also very good at plant arrangements with summer-flowering annuals. France has had the custom of *Villes et Villages Fleuris* for many years: towns and villages compete to make their public spaces the most beautiful. Countless alluring combinations feature on roundabouts, along verges, in tubs of flowers, and borders in large and small parks—combinations which provide endless inspiration for garden enthusiasts. But councils in the Netherlands should also go and look at them sometime; it would be to their advantage.

My plans are based on a number of these French arrangements. You see, I am regularly engaged by a Dutch company which exports bulbs to France and offers its regular customers ready-made plans in which flower bulbs and perennials or summer-flowering annuals are combined into colourful arrangements. It's always great fun devising these arrangements, because the possibilities are endless: single-colour borders, multi-coloured borders, borders with plenty of structured plants, with ornamental grasses, imposing or sweet and charming borders... more than enough to choose from.

Arnhem in the Netherlands is a city which looks beyond the obligatory beds of evergreen ground cover such as *Cotoneaster* and aims for a more colourful, diversified look in the city centre. A few years ago, the council asked me to design a 'green lung' in the centre of the city. The instructions were to come up with plans for alternating plants (spring-flowering bulbs and summer-flowering annuals) for various borders and beds lying in a line alongside a busy main road through the city. After a number of successful years, beds were added around the town hall and a few tubs of flowers were placed at various points in the centre. The reactions from the city's residents indicated that they were delighted with the additional colour throughout the seasons.

Inspiration

But I don't just find inspiration from gardens, nurseries, and public green spaces. Nature itself, with its often-curious patterns and artistic structures created by wind or other circumstances, will inspire you just as much if you pay attention to it. You will see patterns of natural perfection from which you can learn things about space and proportions. You can see the same near-naturalness in good architecture, such as that of Mucem, a new museum in Marseilles, for example. The building's façades seem to be made of lace, with intriguing, sometimes repetitive patterns you can't stop looking at. You know instinctively that it is exactly right in all its simplicity—the same feeling you get when suddenly, after sketching a design or puzzling over arrangements for hours, you know that it is perfect: sheer joy!

Part of the inspiring façades of the Mucem in Marseilles

You can bring nature a bit closer by planting the roofs of office buildings and multi-storey car parks—even more so if you use plants which attract butterflies and bees, such as *Allium senescens* and *Agastache*.

At a high level!

August is also the time to visit my own projects once again. I never have time in spring or early summer. Two things vie for my attention in those seasons: the garden, for one, which I walked through every day on the way to my place of work and where something always needs doing. And the other is the projects I do for other people: March, April, and May are always very busy months, and the work can sometimes run into June and July. So that only leaves August for other business because my calendar is full again in September.

Sometimes I develop projects from beginning to end by myself, and sometimes I come in halfway through, such as when a landscape architect or an agency asks for my expertise on the topic of planting arrangements. I've worked on a number of projects in that way with Michael van Gessel and Francien van Kempen. One of the most recent was the planting plan for roof gardens on top of the new headquarters of ASR in Utrecht, a project belonging to Jeroen van Schooten. The building has three floors, each with its own meticulously devised colour scheme for the interior: yellow, orange, and dark purple.

The colour in the outdoor area had to match the interior on each floor, and we started by laying out the yellow roof terraces. The client's

instructions were to keep to the main colour and to create something that is attractive virtually all year round and that requires as little maintenance as possible. To link the three roof terraces together, all of them were planted with 55% ornamental grasses (Nassella *tenuissima* and *Panicum virgatum* 'Rehbraun'), and *Anthemis tinctoria* 'Wargrave Variety', *Rudbeckia fulgida* var. *deamii, Euphorbia cyparissias* 'Clarice Howard', and *Crocosmia × crocosmiiflora* 'George Davison' were added to the yellow terraces. Because the yellow roof terraces are at the highest level, and their background is distant office buildings, the skyline of Utrecht, and blue or grey skies, it is almost as if you are looking out across a sunny, practically luminous flower meadow. But the other, lower levels have their own charm too: the ornamental grasses on the purple roof terraces are accompanied by *Salvia nemorosa* 'Caradonna', *Geranium* 'Rozanne', *Allium senescens*, and *Verbena bonariensis*. They make these roof terraces a paradise for bees and butterflies. The plants chosen to complement the grasses on the sheltered orange roof terraces are *Asclepias tuberosa, Geum* 'Dolly North', and *Crocosmia* 'Emily McKenzie' and 'Fire King'.

I designed a roof terrace years ago for the headquarters of Cisco along the A9 motorway in southeastern Amsterdam, but the setting was completely different: on top of a semi-underground car park and embraced on three sides by high, terracotta-coloured office buildings. Perennials in shades of purple dominated here—the interplay between them and the

buildings behind them proved to be fantastic. Elements of this planting plan included *Verbena bonariensis, Agastache* 'Blue Fortune', and *Astrantia major* 'Claret'. Here, ornamental grasses were a feature and included *Calamagrostis* × *acutiflora* 'Overdam', Nassella *tenuissima*, and *Pennisetum alopecuroides* 'Hameln'.

Now, almost 15 years later, these features have become the main act. Hardly any colour is provided by flowering perennials anymore, and the species originally planted have all been replaced over the years by other species of ornamental grasses. We are unlikely to find out whether they were lost or whether it was due to management. What is certain is that good management over a long period is essential in all cases. And often things go wrong because 'it is up to the manager'. I count myself lucky in this case because apparently the manager has taken account of the plant arrangement and has given it his own twist without destroying my original plan. It now looks more austere, but it is still imposing.

Signs with names of plants are indispensable but should not detract from the plants, so I come up with creative solutions.

Visitors

Our garden attracts the most visitors in spring when the bulbs are in full flower. But even in summer months, groups of cyclists and hikers regularly come to have a look at the garden on fine days. If I'm working in the garden, I'm always approached cautiously for the names of certain plants ... and asked why there aren't any name tags—a fair enough question, in theory. I've tried to work with name tags in all sorts of ways, but those methods didn't work.

Our garden is an example of what a private garden might look like; it isn't a botanical garden in which all the different species have a name and can be examined. To allow the garden's character to be expressed as much as possible, you want to place the name tags such that they don't disturb the overall picture—unobtrusively, in other words—but then they quickly become overgrown. The option I have now chosen is to place a name on one spot where a lesser-known plant has just come into flower. So I put one next to *Cardamine heptaphylla* in spring, for example, and next to *Gladiolus murielae* in summer. I write the name on a tiny upside-down plant pot set on a bamboo stake. The name can then be read easily, and I can get on with my work, because there is usually more than enough to do.

12 Months in My Garden

JANUARY

FEBRUARY

MAY

JUNE

SEPTEMBER

OCTOBER

MARCH

APRIL

JULY

AUGUST

NOVEMBER

DECEMBER

Euphorbia schillingii

Favourite Plants: Coloured Leaves

You need foliage plants to add a note of sobriety, of intensification, or as a feature amongst all the colours and shapes which determine the content of a border. You could arrange ornamental grasses under foliage plants because they are so different in appearance than border plants, but in this case the focus is on plants with unusual foliage. Their shape, colour, and size, but usually a combination of the three have determined my final decision:

Aralia cordata 'Sun King'

Brassica oleracea 'Redbor'

Brunnera macrophylla 'Sea Heart'

Carex comans 'Bronco'

Heuchera villosa

Ipomoea batatas 'Margarita'

Perilla frutescens

Rubus odoratus

Trachystemon orientalis

FLORAL BORDER, AMERONGEN CASTLE

The flower garden at Amerongen Castle consists of ten borders, each with an area between 20 and 25 m². This sort of size can easily be transposed to a private garden. The basis for the borders is formed by shrubs that will not grow too big, such as *Perovskia* and *Lespedeza*. Perennials feature largely, complemented by ornamental grasses. As far as possible, we chose perennials that are attractive to look at in winter too, either because they are evergreen (*Helleborus, Geum*) or because they have a characteristic silhouette in winter, such as *Sedum* and *Agastache*. In conjunction with ornamental grasses such as *Pennisetum* and *Carex*, the perennials ensure that there is still something to admire in the winter months.

We chose warm colours: red, orange, deep blue, and purple. These colours are replicated as much as possible in the spring-flowering bulbs (*Tulipa* 'Don Quichotte', 'Recreado', 'Ballerina', and 'Couleur Cardinal') and in the dahlias which are planted in May every year as an additional feature in amongst the perennials. Dahlias like 'David Howard' (orange) and 'Karma Lagoon' (magenta) are wonderful eye-catchers in summer. This combination of spring-flowering bulbs, perennials, and summer-flowering bulbs ensures that the garden displays a succession of colour combinations from early spring well into autumn. Although it becomes a little more subdued in the first months of winter, the display still has an obvious structure.

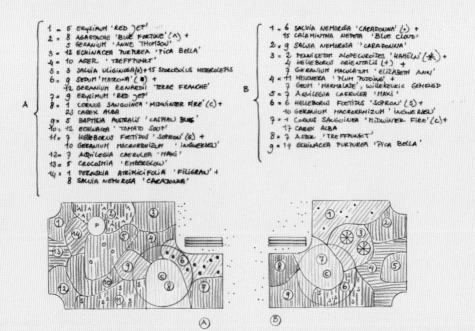

MY FAVOURITE COMBINATIONS

Here I will share my favourite combinations of bulbs. In these photo galleries I hope you can see the beauty and magic of colours, shapes, texture, and character when paired in tandem in the garden. I have suggested percentages to give a guidepost for how many of each variety to plant, but feel free to adjust it according to your own vision.

Daffodil Combinations

Narcissus 'Elka' (60%), *Muscari* 'Baby's Breath' (40%)

Narcissus 'Geranium' (orange crown, 50%), *Narcissus* 'Sailboat' (white with yellow trumpet, 25%), *Narcissus* 'Thalia' (white, 25%)

Narcissus 'Waterperry' (50%), *Narcissus* 'Yellow Cheerfulness' (50%)

Daffodil Combinations

Narcissus 'Jenny' (50%), *Muscari latifolium* (50%)

Narcissus 'Hawera' (55%), *Tulipa bakeri* 'Lilac Wonder' (45%)

Narcissus 'Thalia' (white, 35%), *Narcissus* 'Salome' (white with apricot trumpet, 30%), *Narcissus* 'Geranium' (white with orange crown, 35%)

Daffodil Combinations

Narcissus 'Jack Snipe' (white with yellow, 25%), *Narcissus* 'Minnow' (yellow, 25%), *Muscari latifolium* (light and dark blue, 15%), *Muscari armeniacum* (blue, 15%), *Muscari armeniacum* 'Valerie Finnis' (pale blue, 15%), *Tulipa kolpakowskiana* (5%)

Narcissus 'Jack Snipe' (white with yellow, 35%), *Narcissus* 'Hoopoe' (yellow with orange, 35%), *Muscari macrocarpum* 'Golden Fragrance' (25%), *Fritillaria imperialis* 'The Premier' (5%)

Tulip Combinations

Tulipa 'Jewel of Spring' (yellow, 45%), 'Orange Emperor' (orange, 30%), *Tulipa praestans* 'Shogun' (orange, 25%)

Tulipa 'Maureen' (white, 35%), 'Renown' (pinkish red, 35%), 'Queen of Night' (deep purple, 30%)

Tulipa 'Ballerina' (orange, 40%), 'Daydream' (orange yellow, 40%), 'West Point' (yellow, 20%)

Tulip Combinations

Tulipa 'Black Hero' (deep purple, 30%), 'White Triumphator' (white, 30%), *Narcissus* 'Blanc Double Parfum de Neige' (white, 20%), *Camassia leichtlinii* 'Caerulea' (pale blue, 20%)

Tulipa 'Couleur Cardinal' (red, 40%), 'Carnaval de Nice' (white and red, 20%), 'Verona' (cream white, 40%)

Tulipa 'Flashback' (yellow, 20%), 'Ballerina' (orange, 30%), 'Aladdin' (red with yellow, 30%), *Tulipa orphanidea* (orange, 20%)

Tulip Combinations

Tulipa 'Ballade' (purplish red with white, 40%), 'Purple Dream' (purple, 35%), 'Mistress' (pink, 25%)

Tulipa 'Apricot Beauty' (apricot, 65%), *Narcissus* 'Geranium' (35%)

Tulipa 'Carnaval de Nice' (red and white, 34%), 'Leo' (red, 33%), 'Couleur Cardinal' (red, 33%)

Tulip Combinations

Tulipa 'Christmas Dream' (pink, 18%), 'China Pink' (pink, 18%), 'Peach Blossom' (pink, 18%), 'Rosalie' (pale pink, 18%), 'Orange Emperor' (orange, 18%), 'Easter Moon' (pale yellow, 10%)

Tulipa 'Juliette' (yellow with red, 50%), *Narcissus* 'Water-perry' (cream white and pale yellow, 25%), *Narcissus* 'Yellow Cheerfulness' (pale yellow, 25%)

Tulipa 'Leo' (red, 50%), 'Flaming Spring Green' (white with red and green, 50%)

Tulip Combinations

Tulipa 'Yellow Purissima' (yellow, 30%), 'Purissima' (white, 30%), 'Purissima Blonde' (white, 30%), 'Aladdin' (red with yellow, 10%)

Tulipa 'Ronaldo' (deep red, 35%), 'Yonina' (red with white, 35%), 'Capri' (red, 15%), 'Très Chic' (white with red, 15%)

Tulipa 'Carnaval de Nice' (white and red, 40%), 'Queen of Night' (dark purple, 10%), 'Burgundy Lace' (pinkish red, 10%), 'Spring Green' (white and green, 40%)

Tulip Combinations

Tulipa 'Black Hero' (deep purple, 30%), 'White Triumphator' (white, 30%), *Narcissus* 'Blanc Double Parfum de Neige' (white, 20%), *Camassia leichtlinii* 'Caerulea' (pale blue, 20%)

Tulipa 'Canasta' (red and white, 15%), 'White Parrot' (white, 15%), 'Maureen' (white, 25%), 'Black Hero' (deep purple, 25%), *Narcissus* 'Petrel' (white, 20%)

Tulipa 'Golden Parade' (yellow, 20%), 'Spring Green' (white and green, 20%), *Narcissus* 'Thalia' (white, 40%), *Muscari armeniacum* 'Valerie Finnis' (pale blue, 20%)

Tulip Combinations

Tulipa 'Happy Generation' (white and red, 30%), 'Maureen' (white, 15%), 'Ronaldo' (deep purple, 20%), 'Ballerina' (orange, 35%)

Tulipa saxatilis (lilac, 40%), *Muscari armeniacum* (blue, 60%)

Tulipa 'West Point' (yellow, 35%), 'Marilyn' (whitish + red, 15%), *Narcissus* 'Geranium' (50%)

Tulip Combinations

Tulipa 'Juliette' (yellow, and red, 30%), 'Princesse Charmante' (red, 55%), *Narcissus* 'Geranium' (15%)

Tulipa 'Angélique' (pinkish, 15%), 'Inzell' (white, 35%), 'Garden Party' (white and pinkish red, 15%), 'Mondial' (white, 35%)

Tulipa 'Leo' (red, 40%), 'Flaming Spring Green' (white with green and red, 60%)

Tulip Combinations

Tulipa 'Menton' (apricot pink, 35%), 'Negrita' (lilac purple, 30%), 'Spring Green' (white and green, 35%)

Tulipa 'Mistress' (pink, 40%), 'Temple of Beauty' (pinkish red, 20%), 'Lighting Sun' (pinkish red, 40%)

Tulipa 'Purissima' (white, 50%), 'Flaming Purissima' (shades of pink, 50%)

Tulip Combinations

Tulipa 'Purissima' (white, 15%), 'White Triumphator' (white, 15%), 'Verona' (cream white, 15%), 'Spring Green' (white and green, 15%), 'Très Chic' (white and red, 15%), 'Couleur Cardinal' (red, 10%), 'Carnaval de Nice' (white and red, 15%)

Tulipa 'Wirosa' (red and white, 35%), 'Purissima' (white, 30%), 'Candy Club' (white, 35%)

Tulipa 'Mondial' (white, 20%), 'Negrita' (lilac purple, 20%), 'Shirley' (white with purple, 20%), 'Van Eijk' (pinkish, 20%), 'Menton' (apricot pink, 20%)

Tulip Combinations

Tulipa 'Purple Flag' (purple, 20%), 'Mata Hari' (white with pinkish red, 20%), 'Pays Bas' (white, 10%), 'Pink Diamond' (pink, 20%), 'Queen of Night' (deep purple, 10%), *Tulipa bakeri* 'Lilac Wonder' (lilac, 20%)

Tulipa 'Purple Dream' (purple, 20%), 'Negrita' (lilac purple, 20%), 'Ronaldo' (deep purple, 20%), 'Black Parrot' (deep purple, 20%), 'Maureen' (white, 20%)

Tulipa 'Prinses Irene' (orange, 20%), 'Purple Prince' (purple, 40%), 'Princesse Charmante' (red, 40%)

Dahlias, Alliums, and Other Bulb Combinations

Allium aflatunense 'Purple Sensation' (55%), *Allium* 'Globemaster' (30%), *Camassia cusickii* (15%)

Allium 'Gladiator' (purple, 30%), *Allium* 'Mount Everest' (white, 35%), *Allium* 'Summer Drummer' (buds, 35%)

Anemone blanda 'Blue Shades' (50%), *Muscari botryoides* 'Album' (50%)

Dahlias, Alliums, and Other Bulb Combinations

Crocus vernus 'Flower Record' (35%), *Chionodoxa forbesii* 'Pink Giant' (30%), *Muscari azureum* (35%)

Anemone blanda 'White Splendour' (35%), *Muscari aucheri* 'Blue Magic' (35%), *Scilla bifolia* (30%)

Chionodoxa sardensis (40%), *Narcissus* 'Little Gem' (20%), *Tulipa turkestanica* (40%)

Dahlias, Alliums, and Other Bulb Combinations

Camassia leichtlinii 'Caerulea' (15%), *Tulipa* 'White Triumphator' (30%), *Tulipa* 'Spring Green' (30%), *Tulipa* 'Black Hero' (25%)

Anemone blanda 'Blue Shades' (60%), *Fritillaria michailovskyi* (40%)

Anemone blanda 'Blue Shades' (45%), *Muscari botryoides* 'Album' (45%), *Muscari latifolium* (10%)

Dahlias, Alliums, and Other Bulb Combinations

Dahlia 'Babylon Rose' (40%), *Dahlia* 'Happy Single Wink' (40%), *Liatris spicata* 'Kobold' (20%)

Chionodoxa luciliae 'Alba' (60%), *Fritillaria uva-vulpis* (40%)

Crocus vernus 'Jeanne d'Arc' (60%), *Chionodoxa forbesii* 'Blue Giant' (40%)

Dahlias, Alliums, and Other Bulb Combinations

Dahlia 'Striped Ambition' (deep pink, 20%), *Dahlia* 'Stolze von Berlin' (pink pompon, 25%), *Dahlia* 'Happy Single Princess' (light pink, 20%), *Liatris spicata* (35%)

Dahlia 'Karma Choc' (50%), *Gladiolus murielae* (only foliage, flowers come later, 50%)

Dahlia 'Giraffe' (60%), *Dahlia* 'Golden Scepter' (40%)

Dahlias, Alliums, and Other Bulb Combinations

Muscari armeniacum 'Saffier' (40%), *Hyacinthoides hispanica* 'Rosea' (20%), *Tulipa* 'Queen of Night' (25%), *Fritillaria imperialis* 'The Premier' (15%)

Fritillaria persica 'Ivory Bells' (30%), *Tulipa* 'Angélique' (20%), *Tulipa* 'Burgundy' (30%), *Tulipa* 'Synaeda Blue' (20%)

Muscari armeniacum (80%), *Tulipa* 'Scarlet Baby' (20%)

Dahlias, Alliums, and Other Bulb Combinations

Dahlia 'Requiem' (purple red, 15%), *Dahlia* 'Blue Record' (deep pink, 20%), *Lilium* 'Triumphator' (15%), *Liatris spicata* (40%), *Gladiolus murielae* (10%)

Dahlia 'Moonfire' (50%), *Dahlia* 'David Howard' (50%)

Fritillaria raddeana (40%), *Crocus tommasinianus* 'Ruby Giant' (60%)

Dahlias, Alliums, and Other Bulb Combinations

Muscari armeniacum (blue, 25%), *Muscari* 'White Beauty' (40%), *Tulipa* 'Peppermint Stick' (35%)

Ipheion uniflorum 'Alberto Castillo' (40%), *Muscari* 'Baby's Breath' (60%)

Scilla mischtschenkoana (50%), *Hyacinth orientalis* 'Blue Festival' (50%)

ACKNOWLEDGEMENTS

Writing acknowledgements tends to feel a bit like an obligation. You think that the long process of writing, rewriting, reading it through hundreds of times, dotting the Is and crossing the Ts is over, and then this has to be done on the tail end. When I read a book myself, I often skip over the acknowledgements, because usually you get bogged down in an endless list of names which mean nothing to the average reader.

On the other hand, the result of writing this book—a process which has taken almost 4 years—is not just to my credit. The main driver in the background was my agent and publisher, Hélène Lesger, who continuously and indefatigably read all I had written and suggested adjustments, came up with new ideas and intervals, gave me a push at times when my inspiration was ebbing away, and, in addition to all her other activities, kept such a close eye on the complete process that a book has now appeared that we are both very proud of. So, my greatest thanks go to her.

Immediately next in line is Makenna Goodman, senior garden editor at Timber Press, who started by telling Hélène and me that she was very much interested in another book of mine after *Growing Bulbs in the Natural Garden*. Sometimes a person has all the luck in the world, so thank you, Makenna.

A third person I want to thank is Roy Diblik, a friend for almost 20 years and someone I value very much for his way of thinking—especially his thinking about plants. He immediately agreed when I asked him to write a foreword, and I think he has done a great job; I truly feel honoured.

Last but not least, I want to thank everyone who has contributed to the building blocks which have made this book what it has become, for instance, all the photographers who supplied the missing necessary images, including colleagues such as Piet Oudolf and Cor van Gelderen, and Wouter Eertink, who did the original layout and who was always willing to adapt and change.

These acknowledgements—which I hope are worth reading—mark the real end of this book. But I am already looking forward to writing the next one!

PHOTO CREDITS

Photography by Jacqueline van der Kloet, with the exception of:

INDEX

JACQUELINE VAN DER KLOET is an internationally acclaimed garden designer and one of Holland's best-known gardening authorities, whose advice is sought by designers and landscape architects around the world. Her designs are prized for their beauty, naturalised schemes, and bold uses of colour. Van der Kloet's client list includes some of the most prestigious public gardens in the world, including Holland's famous Keukenhof. In North America, she teamed with Piet Oudolf for innovative plantings at New York's Battery Park, the New York Botanical Garden, and Chicago's Lurie Garden. Her work includes many private gardens as well, and she frequently contributes to international exhibitions. She is the author of *Growing Bulbs in the Natural Garden*.